WHEN
THE MENTAL PATIENT
COMES HOME

CHRISTIAN CARE BOOKS

Wayne E. Oates, Editor

1 When Your Parents Divorce
   William V. Arnold

2 When the Mental Patient Comes Home
   George Bennett

3 Coping with Physical Disability
   Jan Cox-Gedmark

4 After Suicide
   John H. Hewett

5 The Two-Career Marriage
   G. Wade Rowatt, Jr., and Mary Jo Brock Rowatt

6 Coping with Difficult People
   Paul F. Schmidt

COVERING BOOKS 1-6

Pastor's Handbook, Vol. I
Wayne E. Oates

7 Mid-Life Crises
   William E. Hulme

8 Understanding Aging Parents
   Andrew D. Lester and Judith L. Lester

9 For Grandparents: Wonders and Worries
   Myron C. Madden and Mary Ben Madden

10 Coping with Abuse in the Family
    Wesley R. Monfalcone

11 Parents of the Homosexual
    David K. Switzer and Shirley A. Switzer

12 Parents and Discipline
    Herbert Wagemaker, Jr.

COVERING BOOKS 7-12

Pastor's Handbook, Vol. II
Wayne E. Oates

WHEN
THE MENTAL PATIENT
COMES HOME

by

George Bennett

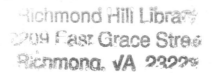

THE WESTMINSTER PRESS
Philadelphia

03-212

1953

Scripture quotations from the Revised Standard Version
of the Bible are copyrighted 1946, 1952, © 1971, 1973
by the Division of Christian Education of the National
Council of the Churches of Christ in the U.S.A., and are
used by permission.

Book Design by Dorothy Alden Smith

First edition

Published by The Westminster Press®
Philadelphia, Pennsylvania

PRINTED IN THE UNITED STATES OF AMERICA
9 8 7 6 5 4 3 2

Library of Congress Cataloging in Publication Data

Bennett, George, 1931–
    When the mental patient comes home.

    (Christian care books ; 2)
    Bibliography: p.
    1. Mentally ill—Rehabilitation. 2. Mentally ill—Home care. I. Title. II.
Series.
RC439.5.B46   362.2'4   79-23809
ISBN 0-664-24295-2

Dedicated to My Parents,
Romeo and Imogene Franklin Bennett,
the importance of whose teachings by word and deed continues
to grow and sustain me and all of those for whom I have the
privilege of caring.

Contents

Acknowledgments   9

Introduction   11

  1. Nobody Is Helpless, Nobody Hopeless   15

  2. Do Half of the Work   18

  3. Dealing with Guilt   23

  4. Relating to Persons and Feelings   28

  5. Focusing on Problems and Facts   39

  6. Tolerating Silence   45

  7. Handling Overactivity   50

  8. Forget What Lies Behind   57

  9. Remember the Past   65

 10. Discerning the Sense in Nonsense   71

Continued

11. Don't Keep Secrets   78

12. When You Have Made a Mistake   87

13. Facing the Threat of Relapse   93

14. Preventing Suicide and Homicide   98

15. Coping with Suicide and Homicide   104

16. Love Life and Let Live   111

*Brief Bibliography of Writings by and Regarding
Convalescent Mental Patients*   117

Acknowledgments

There are so many to whom I owe gratitude. I cannot name them all. Relatives, teachers, friends, students, pastors, doctors, nurses, social workers, faculty colleagues—so many; I shall name but a few. These include Dr. Wayne E. Oates, Chaplains Clarence Barton, Ed Dixon, Wes Monfalcone, Jan Cox-Gedmark, Bill Sapp, James Dent, Darrell Tiller, Powel Royster, and Isaac Njuguna.

I also include Martha Johnson, Brett Mouron, Jim Gilliland, Rick Young, Jay Warthen, Linda Chase, Mark Barnes, John Kirstein, Robert Gardner, Steve Scott, Karen Kokles, Kent Hollingsworth, Forrest and Sue Krummel, Bob Burdett, Janet and Mike Ruark, Pat Clark, and Dr. Lovick C. Miller.

Introduction

The purpose of this book is to provide practical guides for the families, friends, employers, co-workers, and others who wish to relate helpfully to persons who are suffering from and recovering from mental illness and who, perhaps, have come home from a mental hospital or treatment center. It is also a book that can help the patient and the ex-patient. It is not heavily theoretical. A glance through the table of contents will help readers locate specific sections that will speak to their immediate needs. The first several sections set the tone. The rest of the book offers brief answers to most of the questions we have regarding ourselves and others who have suffered or are suffering emotional and mental disturbance.

There are several ways in which the book can be useful, in addition to improving *our* ability to relate helpfully to the recovering person. It has been written so it can be shared with ex-patients. For example, a reader might discover in a chapter something that she or he has been doing that is helpful. That particular paragraph or chapter can be pointed out to the former patient with a statement such as: "I'm sure I confuse things at times, but what I want to do is expressed right here in this book. When I seem to be doing something else, remind me of this. That will help both of us to realize that we are working together to be more confident, happier, and get more from life." Sometimes seeing something in print clarifies what is going on in a relationship better than hearing or guessing. This is true for most of us, whether we have experienced a mental or an emotional disorder or not.

Another use of this book is for group study. Since so many persons are afflicted at times with psychic disorders, most of us want to learn how to cope more constructively with mental problems. Sunday church school classes from the junior high through adult age level could use this book as a resource or study guide. So much has been done in the area of public education regarding physical health that people in the United States and certain other countries have increased life expectancy by many years through improved hygiene, diets, etc. This kind of help is important in the mental sciences also. Unfortunately, until quite recently, most public education regarding mental health has been of the academic type. Complex matters and rare disorders are taught with little practical application for daily living. This book can begin to balance the academic with the vital practicalities of living in a world where stress and disorder continue despite astounding progress in the mental sciences.

This book may also provide self-help for persons who are having, or have had, a draining emotional upheaval. Naturally, this is not a substitute for conversations, consultations, or counseling with specialists as well as with understanding friends. Nor will reading this book remedy situations that require medical assistance. However, the ideas in this book and the experiences they reflect can assist us as we make our way back to the fullness of life and the abundance of joy we were created to experience.

1. Nobody Is Helpless, Nobody Hopeless

If we are to be helpful to the recovering mental patient, we must accept the basic attitude that *nobody* is totally helpless. No matter how severe a disability may seem, the person suffering it can improve. Granted, persons who have experienced massive damage in their brains, who are profoundly retarded, may seem at first to be totally incapable of helping themselves. A second look, however, reveals that even those with the most debilitating damage can respond to care, love, and firm challenge.

For ten years I served full time in a mental institution operated by the state. It housed persons with all sorts of mental and mental/physical disorders. Through modern scientific treatments and progressive commonsense care, the patient population of that hospital declined from nearly 2,500 to less than 600 in a twenty-five-year period. At the same time, the number admitted for treatment increased tremendously. Many who once were "warehoused" as "incurable" and "hopeless," and were considered to have "lost their minds," now live, work, love, and enjoy life outside the hospital.

There are times when people may seem hopeless. Most of us have experienced the feeling of total helplessness on occasion. There may be times when every one of us needs to be totally cared for—briefly. "Briefly," however, is the key word. We do recover the potential to help ourselves, and the capacity to hope again. How quickly and how completely we make this recovery depends largely on the attitudes of others as they relate to us.

To regard recovering mental patients as helpless and hopeless is to contribute to their disability. A long time ago I learned from a brilliant psychiatrist that "people will only be as responsible as we let them." When we treat people as if they cannot recover, we impede their improvement. On the other hand, realizing that they can grow stronger, increase their potential, and overcome disabilities of the past, we communicate a healthy influence both spiritually and scientifically, and people respond positively.

Psychiatrists on active duty during the war learned that soldiers who "broke down" in combat should not be kept in recovery areas too long. Those who were returned rapidly to active duty did well. Those hospitalized for long periods tended toward further disintegration of personality and ability to function.

The same is true in civilian life. Even those who have brain damage and are not challenged to develop good habits or to learn basic grooming and "civilized" ways of behaving will have increased difficulty in learning to help themselves. Persons who suffer emotional and mental problems and are not expected to improve will show little progress.

So, if we would help the recovering mental patient, we must approach the patient with the basic attitude that nobody is helpless or hopeless. An old slogan in mental hospitals goes: "What you expect you will get." As we expect people to continue recovery, they will recover. This is the most basic contribution we can make to the convalescent mental patient who comes home.

In the chapters that follow, I will provide some practical guidelines for implementing this positive attitude as we care for the convalescent mental patient.

2. Do Half of the Work

Do no more than fifty percent of the work, whatever the task at hand may be. This is a wise rule for relating to a recovering mental patient. It avoids the detrimental extremes of robbing the convalescent of a sense of self-worth, on one hand, or of pushing too severely on the other hand.

A helpful analogy comes from the modern science of surgery. Good postoperative nursing practice involves, among other things, helping the patient to move, turn in bed, sit, stand, and walk soon after surgery. This practice helps the blood system and saves many lives.

The postoperative nursing personnel know that the patient cannot turn, sit, stand, or walk alone at first. So they help. They do half the work. They also know that this is a painful experience for some patients. Therefore, they are kindly supportive, not demanding or pushy. In due time the patient is able to move unassisted, yet still with soreness perhaps. The nurses watch with encouragement, ready to help if needed, not interfering with the patient's progress, *expecting* the patient to improve rapidly. They know from training and experi-

18

ence that nobody is totally helpless or hopeless, except for the brief time of anesthetization and the following hours in the recovery room.

The same techniques are effective with the recovering mental patient. For example, some recovering patients lack the psychic energy to get up out of bed. They seem to want to sleep or lie about for hours or days. Gentle, yet firm assistance that is not coercive or hardhearted will help them to begin to move, sit, stand, and walk.

A common experience with convalescent mental patients is their seeming inability or reluctance to brush their teeth, take a bath, or change clothing. This may symbolize a regression to that earlier age when someone else took responsibility for these things. Or it may represent the convalescent patients' low feelings of self-worth—as if by appearing dirty and unkempt they are letting others know how little self-esteem they really have.

Such patients must be helped to help themselves. Provide a toothbrush, a hairbrush, and other necessities at the patient's bedside and gently challenge the person to use them. Escort the patient to the shower, with the water already running. Have fresh, clean clothing ready to be put on after the shower. These steps encourage the patients to do what should be done and to do it themselves.

The opposite approaches are less productive. To shout, demand, hit, or coerce patients lowers their self-confidence. Throwing up one's arms in despair and muttering something such as, "He's a hopeless slob," has precisely the same effect on the patient. Not many people are shamed into better grooming. The temptation is to wonder what "they" did at the hospital to make him so slovenly; or to think, "She really has lost her mind—she used to be so neat and clean all the time."

What is needed is a firm, yet kindly cooperative effort. Do not "do it all" for them, nor let them lie soiled and neglected. Patients need help and encouragement to generate increased self-confidence and self-esteem.

There are other examples of doing half the work. If a patient is not up to being with the whole family for a time, invite the person to eat meals privately, but insist that it be at the kitchen table, not in the patient's room. When it is time for the person to take a walk, do not push him out the door with a statement such as, "If you don't get out, you *will* go crazy!" Or, if a patient is ready to take a solitary walk, do not suggest, "You'd better stay in. You might get lost, or hurt yourself." To walk along and try to build confidence in the patient are ways of doing "half of the work."

As the convalescent patient improves in ability to participate in the world, it is important to offer encouragement by doing enough and no more. One woman whose husband was ready to go for walks alone did half the work by having him telephone every two hours. By this means both of them felt the security of contact, yet enjoyed emancipation from overdependence and overcontrol. A man whose wife was able to go back to her job but was still fearful of being out alone drove her to the bus stop, saw that she was safely aboard, then met her upon her return. In due time she was able to walk to the bus alone, and later "fight the damn traffic," as she phrased it, as she drove to work herself.

It is fortunate that in helping the convalescent mental patient we can make a number of mistakes without causing irrevocable damage. When we apply too much pressure too soon, become too authoritative or too unsupportive, we quickly learn what works and does not work well in our relationship. The patient will let us know verbally, or by being unable to carry through with the desired goal. One young man was sent by his family to apply for a job. He not only failed to get the job, he also lost his way and could not find the place to apply for it. The family learned from this experience that getting him to the proper place and person was their half of the work; letting him follow through with the interview was his half. They had learned through a mistake just how much half the work was.

In another family the well-intentioned wife accompanied her husband, answered the questions of the prospective employer, and filled out the application form for him. Naturally, he was not hired. When she learned to move into the background and let him fumble through the interview, another employer was impressed with his ability to handle an obviously stressful situation and decided the company could use a person like that. The wife learned what fifty percent of the work was in that situation.

An alcoholic is hurt when attending a party to find that all the strong drink suddenly is hidden; or when pressure is put on by "friends" to have a drink when she or he obviously does not want to "fall off the wagon." In a similar way, a convalescent mental patient needs both the security of friends to help and give support and the confidence-building experience of doing and of making decisions. Since most of us are moved by compassion, as well as by less worthy motives such as one-upmanship, our tendency is to do too much. Some of us, threatened by the appearance of what we have been conditioned to think of as weakness, are tempted unwittingly to be too harsh in what we expect of the convalescent person.

Therefore, we need to learn what no more than half the work is for each person for whom we care. This holds true in child-rearing, marriage, and family relationships, as well as with the convalescent mental patient.

3. Dealing with Guilt

Understanding guilt is important in caring for the mental patient who comes home. Guilt, in simple language, means experiencing a feeling that one has done something wrong. It means feeling badly about one's self. In a sense, guilt means not liking one's self, either because of what one has done or not done, or because of what one is or is not.

There are two kinds of guilt. One is real guilt, which we feel when we have done something wrong: for example, when we intentionally and knowingly do something to hurt someone who does not deserve to be hurt. Sometimes the hurt may be physical, such as hitting or breaking something that someone likes. Children often hit or throw in anger. They may purposefully damage a toy that belongs to another child out of jealousy or selfishness. As children grow older, it is hoped they will learn to curb jealousy and control anger, because they are taught that intentionally hurting someone else or someone else's things is not right.

People may feel hurt if they do not get invited to a party, are not elected to a church office after proving worthy, or are not spoken to. I am always impressed by visitors who come to our offices and speak to all the people in the office—secretaries, janitor, students, patients. Those who notice and speak only to the "big shots" and ignore others hurt the feelings of those others.

There are other ways in which we can do wrong intentionally, knowingly, and uncaringly. The result *should* be that we feel truly guilty and decide not to commit that wrong again. Guilt also leads to apology that is appropriate, a replacing of anything broken or lost, and, in the deepest sense, confession to God.

The second kind of guilt is not true guilt. It is the false guilt that people may experience for not being perfect, for being human, making mistakes, falling short of impossibly high self-expectations. This kind of guilt does not lead to redemption, but leads to deepening self-torture and depression. The person suffering from guilt over not being perfect becomes isolated from others, broods, and experiences emotional pain and loneliness.

Often people develop this second, sick kind of guilt through not understanding things during their childhood. For example, parents who do not want to see their young children's feelings hurt may say things such as, "You don't have to win to enjoy playing games." The child may misunderstand the parents' intention and think: "They don't believe I'm good enough to win—maybe I'm not. I ought to be better." The child then tries harder to be better and better, never satisfied with even superior performance in athletics, schoolwork, job, or marriage. This kind of misunderstanding can lead to severe guilt at not being perfect. The accompanying depression can even lead to suicidal thoughts and attempts based on the feeling, "Since I'm never going to be good enough to please anyone, everyone will probably be better off if I am dead."

Other people develop unhealthy guilt at not being perfect because of *undue* pressures from parents, teachers, and other "grown-ups." In childhood these people may have been expected to behave quietly, as more mature people do—never being boisterous, which is at times normal for children. They may be influenced to feel that it is wrong to want to run, play, shout, laugh, and have fun. As they grow older, any natural inclination to enjoy life feels wrong to them. Taking pleasure in normal enjoyments such as seeing the beauty of nature, exploring the many small mysteries of daily living, toys, art, sex, extra helpings of dessert, joking, and resting—all may seem a sinful waste of time and energy. The impulse to want to enjoy seems an imperfection to such people and is guilt-causing, because others expected too much of them as children.

One of the most common reasons people expect too much too soon from children is that they want children to do well in life. Sometimes this is because of love for the child. Parents often want their children to get more from life and do better in life than they did. Therefore, the parents teach the child not to be satisfied with less than the best.

This may confuse the child who may be able to do a very good job of putting away toys, making a bed, fixing a sandwich —for a small child. Older people could, of course, do a better job. If the child's performance, good for a child's age, is compared to the superior ability of adults, the child will develop self-doubt, self-contempt, and guilt that may last a lifetime. Not being better than can reasonably be expected leads to sick guilt. And sick guilt is one cause of mental illness.

Parents usually give the well-intentioned messages that cause sick guilt by saying something such as the following: "If you can't do better than that, never mind. Here, let me show you how to do it right!" The child is crestfallen. Pride in accomplishment is replaced by guilt at not having done better.

Possibly the most guilt-inducing phrases in the English language are, "Shame on you," or "You ought to be ashamed of yourself." These phrases may be intended to encourage a child to excel for the sake of the child or for the convenience of the parent. The result is often a start on the road to guilt over not being perfect and shame at being human.

What can be done about guilt in order to care better for the convalescing mental patient? Examine the guilt of the person to see if it is deserved, appropriate, or caused by intentional selfish desire to hurt someone else. If so, the person must confess, apologize, make atonement and restitution. The person must repair the damage to others and their possessions, and must reestablish relationships based on renewed, humble commitment not to do the wrong act again.

If the guilt is over not being perfect—perfect parents, perfect children, perfect people—another strategy is indicated. These persons must give up the impossible ideal that perfection is attainable, even desirable, in people, including the self. They must admit to being human, and must accept their need and their right to deserve some time to waste, some pleasure for enjoyment's sake. They need to relax unrealistically high standards of excellence and decide they are not going to be perfect. Even Jesus said, when addressed as "Good," "There is none good but One," referring to God.

Have them say to themselves each day: "I will not be ashamed to be wrong sometimes. God made me human, not divine. Therefore, I will appreciate my imperfections."

In relating to the convalescent mental patient, avoid demanding perfection. Accept such persons for who and what they are. Do not expect them to do more than they are able. Allow them to make reasonable mistakes. Letting live, rather than trying to dominate and control, encourages their growth and health.

Sometimes the family and friends of convalescing mental patients feel guilt themselves. They feel somehow responsible for the illness. This is a subtle form of feeling guilty over not being perfect family members or friends of the patient.

Realizing one's own inevitable imperfections communicates acceptance of the imperfections of the recovering patient. The convalescent mental patient will in time respond with diminished unhealthy guilt, increased self-confidence, and accomplishment. Getting rid of one's own unhealthy guilt inspires recovering patients to get rid of theirs. Then everyone is better, happier, more productive, and more fulfilled.

4. Relating to Persons and Feelings

Our current era focuses on problems. International problems, interpersonal problems, financial problems, health problems, teen-age problems, the problems of the elderly, etc. All are brought to our attention daily by the media.

Facts are also heavily emphasized. "The facts of life" is a phrase often invoked in discussion or arguments. It is a phrase that carries almost unquestionable power. But "facts"—from the bank balance to a bacterial count are half the story of living. Life truly is "greater than logic."

In the care of the convalescent mental patient, problems and facts are important. But more important are personhood and feelings.

For example, a recovering girl patient may feel that she is bad for having gotten sick. Having gone to a hospital for treatment, instead of staying home to work, she has been unable to carry out responsibilities in the family. No doubt her absence does affect the family routine, but what is more important is her health and well-being. Mental illness is as "good" a reason as acute appendicitis for going to a hospital,

28

but appendicitis would not be likely to arouse the same feelings of guilt. What she needs most of all is to be affirmed as a person. Therefore, do not respond to her problem by saying something such as: "Yes, you really let us all down. But then, you've always been a problem." Instead, say something that recognizes the problem *and* responds to her as a person. Such a statement might be as follows: "We missed you very much during your hospitalization. You are important to us, sick or well, and I'm glad you are well enough to be back home."

In such circumstances it is important to accept the feelings of the patient as well as to recognize the facts. When the patient complains of feeling guilty for having deserted the family, a helpful response would not ignore the feelings of the person. Neither would it add to the guilt. Saying: "Don't even *think* of feeling guilty, you poor thing! You are wrong to feel guilty over deserting the family to rest in the hospital! That is just feeling sorry for yourself. Shame on you for feeling that way. Why, it is a fact that a lot of weak people can't make it without drugs and psychiatrists. You're just one of them, so I don't want to hear any more about you feeling guilty!" Saying something like the above will obviously make the convalescing patient feel worse. She will be made more isolated, and have greater trouble communicating her feelings. She will doubt herself, be ashamed, withdraw from talking, and become increasingly lonely.

A more helpful kind of response would be along the following lines: "I'm sure you do feel guilty at having to be away. Factually, of course, being ill and hospitalized is not a sin or a crime, but you still feel guilty and that is probably quite normal under these circumstances. I'm sorry you feel guilty when there is no realistic reason to, but I am glad you are able to talk about it with me. Tell me, if you wish, more of how you feel."

There are times when it is quite difficult to relate to the convalescing patient at the level of person and feelings. Often these are times when the recovering patient has ideas, feelings, hopes, and desires that are quite *different* from those of a friend or a family member. For example, consider the following conversation between a father and his son who had been recently discharged from a mental hospital.

FATHER: Well, it's certainly good to have you back home and ready to go back to college. After all, you can't get on with your commerce degree and become a banker like your dad while you are in the hospital!

SON: Ah, yes. I'm glad to be out of the hospital too. Only I'm not sure I'm, well, really ready to go back to college.

FATHER: What? But of course you feel you are ready to go back to college! Why, that's what we have always wanted for you. You know the facts of life—you just can't make it in the business world without a college degree these days! What did they tell you up at that damn hospital anyway?

SON: Dad, it isn't anything anybody told me there or anywhere. It's just that, well, I know the facts of life. I know I need college if I'm going to make a lot of money the way you have. And I know money is important. It's just that, well, I really have always wanted to do something else with my life. You remember how I enjoyed being in the Sea Scouts? Well, I've always liked boats and the water. There is something so, well, peaceful, so powerful, so, so, well, great and wonderful, about the rivers and lakes and seas.

FATHER: Yes, that's all very well and good, but it doesn't put food on the table. Besides, bankers are great at fishing. Why, some of my associates spend a lot of time —and waste a lot of money, if you ask me—going fishing. Wanting to play Sea Scout all your life doesn't sound very good as a long-term investment to me.

SON: No, Dad, please. I don't mean I want to play Sea Scout the rest of my life. I mean I've been thinking about, well, enlisting in the Navy.

FATHER: Now that is dumb. Oh, you young people. Listen, I was *in* the service during the war. Believe you me, that *is* a waste. Oh, sure we need all the national security we can have, but there are plenty of dumb kids around who couldn't hack it in college or business—they make good soldiers and sailors. They also rip us honest hard workers off when it comes to the tax dollar! No, you don't want to go in the service.

SON: Dad, I really think I do. Besides, you've always talked about how important it is for young people to try their wings, be on their own, cut the apron strings. Maybe the Navy could be just the thing. If not, I could go back to college later.

FATHER: And waste time when you could be building a future that amounts to something. You know, if you really are dead set on this Navy thing, all the more reason to finish college. Then you could go in as an officer. Not bad pay with promotions and such. And, twenty short years and you could retire and begin business with a guaranteed income. So, sounds like back to college for you, huh?

SON: (Begins to stare vacantly into space, with an expression of mild pain on his face)

FATHER: Son! What's wrong? Why are you looking like that?

SON: Huh? Oh, sorry, Dad. I was just, just . . . I don't know.

The above conversation illustrates how one person has a difficult time relating to the personhood and feelings of another who has a totally different attitude and outlook. The result is disappointing broken communication. In the conversation recorded above, neither the father nor the son was wrong in any way. Each had reasonable ideas as to what is important in life. For the father, a successful career in business was the best he could hope for his son. Money *is* important in this life. College is necessary ordinarily for a young man to move up the "ladder of success." These facts and attitudes are the real, practical, foundations of the American economic system which has brought so much to so many.

On the other hand, the son seemed to have been able to think through his own attitudes toward life. The lure, mystery, adventure, almost religious sense of the sea was far more meaningful to him than college at present. He knew how he felt. His feelings were stronger than the financial facts of banking. He also had a practical plan—to enlist in the Navy and see whether his feelings and attitudes would stand the test of time, or whether they were simply remains of late childhood fantasy. He knew he was young and could still have a career in business if his experience in the service proved unfulfilling.

He was actually more aware of the true meaning of his father's teachings that young people should launch out on their own than the father who had taught one thing ("Be on your own") at one time, and another ("Do as I say") at another.

To repeat, neither of the two was wrong. They were simply on different "frequencies" or "channels," in radio and television jargon. Thus, responding to person and feeling was difficult because of the difference in attitude, opinion, and a sense of what is most important in life.

There is another common reason why people have difficulty relating at the person and feeling level rather than at the problem and fact level. There are times when the convalescent mental patient may be aware of and talk about feelings that family and friends inwardly have but do not know they have.

For example, most people think about or feel like committing suicide at one time or another. Killing one's self is considered bad, a sin, crazy, in our part of the world. Therefore, most people put such thoughts out of their minds as quickly and completely as possible. I often hear people make statements such as: "I can't imagine what gets into someone who commits suicide. I love life, miserable as it is, too much to even *think* of such a dreadful thing!" Upon being questioned, such people almost inevitably will concede that there *have* been times when they thought, "I did think maybe everyone would be better off with me dead"; or: "I have gotten so tired of living lately with all my burdens. Sometimes I feel that if I could just have cancer or a heart attack, I'd get some rest." This usually means that the speaker has had or does have suicidal thoughts but does not recognize them as such. The self-destructive urges are "unconscious," to use the term of psychoanalysts.

The communication difficulty in relating to persons and feelings rather than to problems and facts in this instance is caused by fear of one's own unrecognized self-destructive impulses. When someone else speaks of suicide, those who have repressed their own suicidal thoughts will be too uncomfortable to listen to such talk.

Mental patients are ordinarily taught by their doctors and counselors to accept their thoughts and feelings, both positive and negative. This teaching is to help the patients cope more effectively, less destructively, with their impulses, thoughts, and feelings. They are then able to be masters of their emotions rather than slaves to them.

When such patients return to family and friends, they may not realize that family and friends are not prepared to deal with such strong, sometimes fearful feelings and thoughts. Family and friends are confused by such frank talk. They try to avoid conversations about these feelings and thoughts by changing the subject, focusing on problems and facts. This makes the convalescent patient feel wrong, isolated, different.

Some people are able to overcome their own fears out of love and care for the patient. Others may need conversation with qualified counselors. This will help them overcome their own difficulties in confronting and overcoming strong but suppressed feelings. Such feelings include rage, self-destruction, and lust—all the common human emotions. Then they are free to relate to the person and feelings of the convalescent mental patient in a helpful way. The following conversation is typical of one that is helpful in caring for the recovering mental patient:

FRIEND: Hi! Good to see you out of the hospital. I hope you are glad to be back home.

PATIENT: Hello. I guess I am glad to be back. I don't know, though. Sometimes I am afraid to be back out. I felt very secure in the hospital. You know they won't let you do anything to hurt yourself or other people in there. Out here, I don't know. I get so angry sometimes. Sometimes I have the urge to kill someone.

FRIEND: That sounds scary. You are pretty brave to let me know that you have such temptations. I know I have gotten very angry at times with some people. My boss is one example. I sometimes wish she would get run over by a steamroller or fall into a volcano or something. I don't think I'd ever actually try to hurt or kill her, but I've sure thought about it.

PATIENT: I guess that's the difference between us. I'm not sure I *wouldn't* try to hurt somebody. My doctor says so long as I talk about it, talk it out, then I won't. But I'm not sure. I mean, how does the doctor *know* I can talk it out and not do it?

FRIEND: Yeah. I'm not so sure those doctors *can* be trusted to know what they are doing. I don't blame you for wondering.

PATIENT: Oh, it isn't that I don't trust my doctor. My doctor is great. So is my social worker. And the other people in there. I do trust them. In there. Out here, what do they know I might do or not do? I mean, they say I should talk about these things and yet my folks say I shouldn't even think of them, let alone talk about them. What if I can't find somebody to talk it out with?

FRIEND: Well, you have me. And I imagine you could call some of them at the hospital. And there's the pastor at the church, and . . . well, one of us is bound to be available anytime. But that's not how you are feeling, is it? You are feeling that you may get into a rage and not have anybody to talk to, right?

PATIENT: Well, I was feeling that way. But I guess you are right. There are a lot of people I can talk to. I'm glad you are one of them. You seem to know how I feel. You know me as the person I am. You don't try to make me someone I'm not. And then again, maybe I'm like you more than I thought. When we get to talking about killing and hurting and all, well, maybe I wouldn't *really* do anything like that either, like you. So long as I can talk about it.

FRIEND: Is there anything else that helps?

PATIENT: Well, this is really silly. I feel stupid talking about it to you. But you know, those stories on television. The cops and robbers ones, and the old cowboy movies, where they shoot each other all to pieces and all. Well, sometimes if at the end when the good guys win, well, I feel better. I guess I sort of get it out by watching as well as by talking. But that's kid stuff. Dumb!

FRIEND: Then I'm dumb too. Myself, I like the space shows, science fiction with all the laser guns and all. When *they* have a fire fight, I really get a kick out of it. When I watch them, I am sort of ashamed, but I sure have better dreams than when I don't. When I'm all upset I have really bad nightmares. Like one night a few weeks ago, I dreamed of being in a big warehouse with all these dead bodies hanging from meat hooks. God, it was awful! But when I get it out of my system by talking or watching "violence" on TV, I don't have such bad dreams.

PATIENT: Wow! What a horrible dream. You give me the creeps. But, then you're so healthy all the time. Maybe I'm not so nuts after all. I really feel good now. I know I was mad about something before we talked, but that doesn't seem important now. I guess I'll go fill out those job applications. After all, you can't earn a living sitting around talking about being mad all the time. See ya!

In the foregoing conversation, the focus of the friend on the person and feelings of the recovering patient helped the patient. The patient was helped to realize that being angry and contemplating violent acts is not abnormal. This was helpful to the point that the patient felt increased security outside the hospital.

Relating to people and feelings, not just to problems and facts, may be of great help to the convalescent mental patient. Often, a few conversations with a qualified counselor enables people to do this in a way that even the most practical "horse sense" will not.

Therefore, in helping to care for the convalescent mental patient you may do well to get some "help" yourself.

There are times and situations when relating to feelings and personhood may *not* help. The following chapter will clarify this.

5. Focusing on Problems and Facts

There are times when people need to have their feelings heard and their personhood recognized. This was discussed in the preceding chapter. There are other times when expressing feelings, "getting close" emotionally, is *not* helpful. These are times when focusing on problems and facts is more constructive than relating to feelings and personhood.

Convalescent mental patients may have been "overwhelmed" by their feelings prior to or during the acute phase of illness. They may have experienced a flood of feelings that had been too long dammed up. As the emotional barrier that dammed up the feelings broke, the patient may have been swamped by feelings. This "swamping" can cause panic as acute as physical drowning. The patient may literally thrash about with seemingly pointless physical activity, much as a person in deep water may flail wildly in an attempt to swim to safety. The panic and wild activity is a dreadful experience for people who are in danger of physical drowning. The same is true for the patient who is engulfed by overwhelming emotions. Confusion, anxiety, and fear reach an extreme that seems intolerable in either situation.

I know persons who almost drowned when they were young. Even in adult life they are afraid to go near deep water. Sometimes such fears are passed on to children.

In the same way, persons who have experienced overwhelming emotions and have been in fearful panic may need to stay away from the expression of feelings during their convalescence. Just as pushing someone fearful of water into a swimming pool may reactivate all the old apprehensions, so encouraging the expression of feelings may undo the good done by psychiatric treatment.

In such situations, it is well to concentrate on the ordinary, everyday facts and problems of life. For example, patients who have attempted suicide should not be encouraged to dwell on their depressed feelings. In a sense, they have attempted to get away from the panic and confusion of feelings too strong for them to tolerate by trying to end their lives. Do not "help" depressed persons to "get in touch with" their feelings. That may only make them feel worse again. They may then feed on further negative feelings in a downward spiral toward self-destructive behavior.

Another instance when one needs to pay attention to facts and problems rather than to feelings and personhood is in the case of suspicious and distrustful convalescent patients. To encourage them to dwell on their suspicions both supports the distrust and its accompanying fear *and* increases emotional closeness to them. When suspicious people feel that others are getting emotionally close, they become suspicious of those people, wondering what their motives are. They feel that their privacy is being invaded. They become more secretive and increasingly fearful. They need emotional distance in order to feel secure. When their suspicions are given attention, either positively or negatively, those suspicions are supported. They wonder why people want to know more about them. They question why people *insist* that the suspicions are groundless.

An example of a positive reinforcement of suspicions would sound as follows: "I would never have noticed the things you said about the report of the school board. Maybe there *is* something going on down there that they want to keep hushed up. What other evidence do you have? Tell me *all* about it." Negative attention to suspicions often comes out as hollow-sounding but forceful denials of the suspicious person's feelings. An example that is typical would be a statement such as "Don't be silly! The school board isn't plotting anything. Why, they are fine people, elected officials. You can trust them as much as you can trust me! Now just forget all that plot stuff and trust us. You're beginning to sound paranoid!"

In either instance, focusing on the suspicious feelings of the convalescent patient reinforces the suspicions in the patient's thinking. Therefore, it is important to know how to relate to the convalescent patient in ways that are helpful when feelings and personhood should not be emphasized.

With the depressed person, the most effective rule of thumb is, *Don't reward misery.* That is to say, do not listen to lengthy accounts of the patient's guilt, remorse, and low self-worth. When you reward the expressions of misery by listening to them, you only help convalescent patients talk themselves further into despair. If you know that someone is recovering from a depressive illness, *do not ask the person how he or she is feeling.* Say: "Hello." Or, "Tell me how you are handling the problem of paying the hospital bill." Or, "There's a good television show on in a few minutes. Let's watch it together."

Convalescent patients usually respond to the latter kinds of statements with some depressive comment such as: "Oh, hello. I feel terrible. You are so friendly and I am so undeserving of even having you speak to me."

In your reply to this kind of statement, avoid expressing any feelings and instead say something about the television show or the hospital bill problem. Ordinarily these persons again come back with: "I don't feel up to watching television. I've wasted my life already. Watching television with me would be a bad experience for you because I'm so down." Again, acknowledging the facts or the problems is helpful. Say: "Oh, yeah, and that's probably the leftover of your depression. I think the TV program is on channel 3. So let's get the set warmed up."

When patients comment on their inability to handle routine things such as the payment of the hospital bill with statements such as: "Because I could never manage money well"; or, "I shouldn't have had to go to the hospital at all. It was a needless expense, wasted on me. I'm not worth it"

—your response should be factual and problem-centered rather than person-centered. For example, say: "Yeah, money is a problem, all right. Are you willing to talk to the financial counselor at the hospital about the bill? Let's handle it with them while you're getting over the depression. Now about this television program . . ."

With suspicious persons, it is helpful to cut off firmly, but not forcefully, the elaboration of suspicions. Say: "Yeah, I remember you don't trust the school board. Anyway, I'm going to 'agree to disagree' about that. I want to talk about the hospital bill (or the television show)." The convalescent patient will ordinarily want to pursue the suspicions and say something such as, "Of *course*, you don't want to talk about the school board because you know that I'm right, only you don't want to admit it, do you?"

Changing the subject from feelings and the person with convalescent mental patients is difficult. This is because the aftermath of their illness hangs on strongly. It is as if the illness does not want the patient to be well. Firm persistence, however, does pay off in helping the convalescent patient improve. Getting "hooked" into the mire of suspicions or depressive talk does not help.

At times, one must be quite firm. "I'll be glad to talk with you about other things, but not about the school board (or how guilty you feel). If that is all you want to talk about, I'll just be quiet and watch the television."

At times the convalescent patient would rather not relate or communicate verbally at all if he or she cannot repeat symptoms of the illness. This may bring about a lot of silence in a household. Many people find tolerating silence quite difficult. The next chapter will discuss ways in which we can help the convalescent mental patient by learning the whys and hows of tolerating silence.

6. Tolerating Silence

As with most things, silence has its reasons. In order to be helpful to the convalescing mental patient, one must understand the reasons why former patients and others are often quiet.

Some people seem quiet by nature. These are deep-thinking, highly intelligent people whose ideas and feelings are somewhat different from those of the "average" person. Often in childhood they have had insights and ideas which their playmates could not understand and about which their parents worried.

When they spoke of these things, they were met by misunderstanding. Perhaps they were made fun of or mocked. They may have been cautioned "not to have such thoughts."

A typical example was young Thomas Edison, who actually had his ears injured by a railroad official. The official felt that Edison's curiosity and experiments were a foolish waste of time. Later, Edison became an "introverted" person who spent lonely hours in his laboratories, perfecting major inventions of history. He was often quiet and withdrawn, isolated and noncommunicative. At other times, he was dogmatic and intimidating, refusing to cooperate with his colleagues and those who worked under him.

There are others, as mentioned earlier, whose normal child-like exuberance and boisterousness was annoying to parents. These people learned in childhood that somehow what came natural to them—making noise, running, shouting, yelling, playing wildly—was not acceptable to others. Rather than run the risk of being criticized, punished, or having their feelings hurt, they made a decision at an early age to keep to themselves and not share their ideas, thoughts, or feelings. In later life, others may resent or be hurt by their quietness.

Other persons may have gotten into trouble by talking. A typical example is the excited, friendly child who is punished for talking during school hours. At first, the child does not understand why talking, which may have been encouraged at home, is suddenly "bad" at school. The child may retire into silence out of a confusion that lingers *emotionally* long after she or he realizes mentally that talking is appropriate at times but inappropriate on other occasions. To simplify things emotionally, the person may determine to keep quiet and not have to decide when talking is "O.K." or not "O.K."

Others who "get into trouble" by talking include former mental patients who temporarily have problems judging when speaking is all right and when it is not all right. This temporary lack of judgment, which results in "trouble," may cause the patient to decide that silence at all times is the only sure solution to avoid trouble.

I recall riding on a bus while visiting New York City when

I was a tenth-grader. A man failed to realize at which street corner he needed to get off the bus and missed his stop. He began to shout at the driver. He denounced the City Transit Authority in anger. Fortunately, the bus driver was experienced and in a loud voice shouted back at the irate passenger. "Coitisy in Noo Oork, pu-leeze" (making a joke of a then-current popular slogan, "Courtesy in New York" intended for the benefit of tourists). The angry man joined in the laughter of the other passengers and nothing troublesome happened.

I have also known recovering mental patients who did the same kind of relatively harmless thing and ended up in handcuffs for "disturbing the peace." Some recovering mental patients, having experienced the latter, may decide just to keep quiet no matter what happens in order to avoid further trouble. I even know one former patient who walked everywhere despite cold and distance. This was done simply to avoid getting into trouble on a public transit coach. He did not trust his judgment as to when and when not to speak.

There may be other reasons why recovering mental patients may elect not to speak or communicate. In any event, the point of this chapter is to assist the family, friends, and others related to convalescing mental patients in tolerating the silence of patients.

The key to tolerating silence is to recognize that people can be together and communicate care and help, without talk. This is a fact extolled in romantic poetry, Saint Valentine's Day cards, and even Holy Scripture. Talking is but one means of communication. I remember a woman who had been married nearly forty years to a man who worked hard, was kind, yet spoke little.

"I have learned not to need talk from him. Just being together in the house in the evenings has become enough for me. I know other husbands are out at bars, drinking, blowing money, leaving their wives alone to wonder in loneliness whether they are loved or not. We do not have to talk to be together, to feel love. He watches sports on television while I read. No words are exchanged. But we know and feel love, togetherness. I prefer that to shallow chatter."

One is reminded of Psalm 19: "There is no speech, nor are there words; their voice is not heard; yet their voice goes out through all the earth, and their words to the end of the world." Also, in his final hours, Jesus did not ask the disciples to talk with him. Rather, as he went into the garden on the mountain overlooking Jerusalem, he simply requested, "Sit here, while I pray" (Mark 14:32). He went alone, trusting that they were with him, even in silence, as he knelt, "silhouetted against the Great Wheel of the Stars" for his final private communication with his God.

When a former mental patient is silent, the helpful thing is to avoid pushing the patient to speak. Demands that the patient talk are commands that to the patient take great risk. The patient who needs to take time before talking has probably had experiences in which talking led to anger, misunderstanding, scorn, shame, or pain, as demonstrated in the preceding chapter.

The more helpful approach is to accept the quietness of the recovering patient. You need to realize that speaking may be a major effort. Letting the patient know that you would like to talk with him or her, but that you do not insist, can be relaxing to the patient. You will worry, of course, and long to hear words. You can tolerate the silence by realizing its importance to the convalescing person. A few statements made infrequently will let the person know that you care. Thus, you maintain a fragile link of communication.

Frustration may inevitably build up with the silence, even when you understand the need for it. This is where friends and one's own counselors come in. You can tell them of the frustration at the silence. If they are wise, they will share your feelings and help you restore your comprehension of the need for the silence. Having a wise friend and counselor of one's own is the most effective way of helping to care for the convalescent mental patient in many ways.

7. Handling Overactivity

Perhaps more troublesome than tolerating silence is handling the overactivity of some convalescent mental patients. Such patients seem to have had sufficient rest while they were hospitalized and now they have extraordinary energy. They may want to talk all the time, sleep little, pace the floor all hours of the night, and think up dozens of plans, schemes, and projects. They may keep up with all current events, and write long letters to newspaper editors, church and civic leaders, radio and television stations, expressing their "solutions" to all kinds of public issues.

Conversing with them may tend to be one-way monologues. They tirelessly run from subject to subject. At times, they may go into tedious details and at other times oversimplify complex situations with pat solutions.

They may also collect all kinds of materials, tools, art objects, record albums, tin cans, string, boxes, photographic equipment, old doorknobs, discarded newspapers—anything from "rubies to rubbish." They can quickly clutter the typical household with such collections. They may make simple routines, such as preparing a meal or just "getting through" the living room, difficult if not hazardous.

Each collection represents some scheme or plan to "get rich quick" or "save the world." Such schemes are as quickly abandoned as impulsively launched. The "vital balance" between activity and inactivity, effort and rest, talking and listening, seems lost.

At times such exuberant excess is a seeming "rebound" from a time of withdrawn, silent, completely nonproductive behavior. Then family and friends hesitate to set limits on the overactive convalescent. The tendency is for them to tolerate the overactivity and squelch their irritation to the point that they finally are worn out. They may then suddenly and sharply lash out pent-up anger after having "humored" the patient for so long.

Naturally, this switch from tolerance to tantrum is confusing to the already somewhat confused convalescent. He or she may respond by increased overactivity and loudness. Neighbors may be bothered, the family may become frantic. The police may be called. The convalescent patient may go back to the hospital, no longer convalescent but acutely ill again.

On the other hand, patients may collapse emotionally when severely and suddenly confronted. They may go back to the withdrawn, mute, nonproductivity of depression. In this case, the patient again becomes no longer convalescent.

A more helpful approach is for family and friends to begin early to assist the patient in setting limitations. This is to be done firmly, yet gently. Helping to set limits is most effective when you first remind the convalescent that you care for him or her a great deal. You then suggest that you are going to let him or her know when activity is becoming troublesome. In the early stages of convalescence, such an understanding bears long-range rewards for all concerned. Where talking incessantly is the overactive behavior, a conversation such as the following may be repeated daily, if not more often:

CONVALESCENT PATIENT: Wait until you hear what I've discovered. All the problems of the world can be solved if people would only get together and recognize their differences and agree to settle everything. I'm going to write to all the presidents and the pope and the kings of the world and invite them to a meeting with scientists and religious leaders. We can do it here and have a potluck supper and they can sleep in the basements of churches. They can bring sleeping bags, and better still, we could get the Scouts to donate or lend them sleeping bags. I'm going to telephone all the ministers and priests in town and then tomorrow I'll go down to City Hall and I'll talk with the mayor and the chief of police—Police, yes, we'll need security . . .

FAMILY MEMBER: Fred. FRED! Stop a minute and take a breath or two. You're talking so fast I can't keep up. You recall I said I would tell you when you were getting too speeded up? Now sit down at the table and stop a minute.

CONVALESCENT PATIENT: Yes, I remember that, and believe you me I'm grateful for all that you mean and care.

That is exactly why I want you in on this thing from the beginning. I could write the letters and you could address them and help with the telephone numbers. I'll start looking them up now while you go out and buy some stamps—

FAMILY MEMBER: Take two or three more breaths. That's right. You know you were speeding up again. When you go that fast nobody can keep up with you. All your good ideas will be lost and all your efforts will be wasted. You keep sitting there. And help yourself to slow down.

CONVALESCENT PATIENT. All right. I'm sitting. But it's hard to sit still with these great ideas going. You see, as I see it, all the troubles of the world could be solved if we can get the leaders of the—

FAMILY MEMBER: Fred. Now very slowly tell me that you want to slow down so we can both talk. Slowly.

CONVALESCENT PATIENT: Ah, well, I guess I want to talk about this, all this. I . . .

FAMILY MEMBER: Slowly. Repeat after me, "s-l-o-w-l-y." Say it softly and say it slowly.

CONVALESCENT PATIENT: Yes. "S-L-O-W-L-Y." I said it too loudly, didn't I? All right, "s-l-o-w-l-y." (Deep breath.) Yes, that's better. I guess I was chattering on at a pretty fast clip. But then this idea is so exciting that I can't help but get going—

FAMILY MEMBER: Ooops. Slowly. Now catch your breath and I'll catch mine. How about a cup of warm milk with a little melted butter on top? You know you used to like that so much.

CONVALESCENT PATIENT: That does sound good. Besides, I'll need something to drink. I think I forgot to take my medicine. May I go get it now? I'll bring it back. And can I get the telephone book and just look up some of the numbers?

FAMILY MEMBER: Sure. Bring your medication while I fix the milk and you can write numbers down while I fix supper.

Firmly interrupt the convalescent patient's overactive talking. Get his attention. Then help him to recognize the runaway behavior. In time the recovering patient "catches himself" with little help from you other than a special "schoolteacher" look. Eventually, the patient recovers the "vital balance" when it comes to slowing down the rush of ideas or words.

Those close to the overactive convalescent patient should encourage communication with the treatment team to report on the progress of the patient. Often the patient can be encouraged to telephone the doctor to see if some change in medication is indicated before contacting the pope about international problems. Communication with the convalescent patient's social worker, nurse, chaplain, or doctors is important in the recovery process. Waiting until things have "gotten completely out of hand" is less helpful than regular and continued communication.

When disturbing behavior such as noisy nightwalking or collecting clutter becomes the problem, certain firm restrictions should be agreed upon. When the patient cannot avoid pacing at night and keeping the family awake, an increase or change in medication may be needed and the doctor will handle this if notified by patient or family. Quiet night behaviors—writing letters, collecting stamps, etc.—may be tolerable when the patient, even with proper medication, cannot sleep. Compromises are essential. Rigid rules are not helpful, since no one can "make" anyone else sleep. However, people can agree that night activities will be acceptable so long as they are quiet and not disturbing to the household. Although in extreme cases convalescent patients can bring themselves to the point of serious physical collapse through overactivity, many people can survive healthfully with little sleep. Trying to enforce "you must go to sleep" is a lost cause. It creates more anxiety and guilt than compromises about noise level at night.

In a similar way, collections and projects should be negotiated rather than forbidden or allowed to go to the extreme. Certain areas may be designated for collections—the garage, part of the basement, the convalescent's room, a tent in the backyard, the apartment patio, or a utility closet. The convalescent can acquire as much as desired so long as it can all be kept in the designated places and not spill over into the rest of the house. When the collections fill the agreed-upon space, the patient and family members should decide what will go out to make room for new things.

The use of the telephone should also be by agreement—no long-distance calls without first clearing them with the one who pays the telephone bill; no telephoning neighbors or others after ten P.M. or before ten A.M.; etc. The same is true in the use of credit cards.

Having the overactive person's medication regularly reevaluated is important. Gentle but firm agreements about calling the patient's attention to overactive behavior from the time the convalescent comes home from the hospital is important. Setting rules with the patient concerning where and how much may be used, collected, spent, and done is important.

Most important of all, however, is the need to recognize that the overactive person does not really enjoy overactivity. This is true no matter how euphoric, how loud, how much joking and laughter she or he demonstrates. People do not like to be "out of control" even when they seem to insist they want to be. They appreciate a steady, gentle, firm setting of limitations. When their vital balance is recovered, they need feel no embarrassment about their overactive behavior. They will feel resentment toward those who let themselves and others become exhausted or who laughed at them during times of overactivity. They will appreciate those who set reasonable limits and take them seriously.

As you relate with realistic, nonrigid support of persons who are overactive, they respond in the long run with love for love, as balance is recovered.

8. Forget What Lies Behind

The apostle Paul once spoke of "forgetting what lies behind" as he moved forward in his important work. The ability to forget the past is important in caring for the convalescent mental patient.

One reason for forgetting the past is that thinking of past disagreements, regrettable statements or actions makes people feel guilty or angry or both. Guilt, as explained in an earlier chapter, is best let go. Old angers should also be let go. Neither the retention of guilt nor old anger helps in the care of the convalescent mental patient.

As an example, consider the situation of a thirty-one-year-old married woman. She was the mother of two children. Friends and neighbors had always considered her an attractive, alert, honest person who carried out her family responsibilities cheerfully. Early symptoms of a depression began to show up in the form of nervousness, insomnia, a loss of appetite, and restlessness with her "lot" in life as a homemaker.

She expressed her increasing unhappiness to her husband. He did not understand why she was changing in attitude and mood. Both of them felt their relationship had been quite good. They usually agreed on the division of responsibilities for work in their home, how to spend their money, and the care of the children. He worked for a plumbing company, and as his years of experience increased on the job, responsibilities were added. He became more "wrapped up" in his work than in the early years of their marriage. He felt more pressure in his job and did not have as much patience with his wife as he had seemed to demonstrate earlier. He felt that her burdens were lighter since they had been able to afford more conveniences for homemaking and since the children had reached school age.

She felt he lacked sympathy for her as her bewildering symptoms developed. At the time she most needed him, he seemed to pull away from her, to become more distant. She discussed her situation with family members and several friends. They advised her to get a job outside of the home, believing she was becoming upset because she "didn't have enough to do." She acted on their advice and secured work as a filing clerk with a local government agency. Soon she began to return from work later than was expected by her family. She no longer prepared meals and became slovenly in what little housework she did. Moody silence with the family replaced her former cheerfulness. She began drinking alcoholic beverages daily on the way home from work and at home.

When her husband or the children attempted to relate to her, she replied with sarcasm or depressed brief statements such as: "I'm having a bad day. Leave me alone."

Her husband became impatient and stayed chronically grumpy as he did household chores she had formerly done. The children were scolded and spent increased time with baby-sitters, not knowing where their parents were at night or when to expect their return. They only knew that their parents were not out together.

One Friday night she did not come home at all. Her husband returned from some hours spent in a local bar playing coin-operated amusement machines with other customers. He took the baby-sitter home, returned, and went to bed. He awakened in the night and became alarmed that his wife had not returned. He telephoned police and hospitals after checking with family. He could not locate her.

She telephoned the next morning, sounding extremely despondent, asking her husband to drive to a motel in which she had spent the night. He found her suffering from a severe hangover. She confessed to him that she had little memory of the previous night, but thought she had stayed part of the night with a man she had gone drinking with after work.

He was shocked and bewildered, too upset to express the anger he felt. He took her home and for several weeks she tried to return to her former "self." He decided to accept her repentant behavior and hoped the worst was over.

Soon, however, her symptoms resumed. The only time she seemed nervously animated was when talking with friends on the telephone or while at work. With family, she was silently hostile. She resumed her practice of going from work to a bar to drink before returning home. When she was home, her irritable and irresponsible behavior alternated with periods of weeping while drinking.

Another all-night-out prompted her husband to express rage that ended in his slapping her. She broke into heavy sobbing, lamenting her ways, begging his forgiveness. He withdrew from her, saying he would have to think about it.

Each talked with family members and friends during the following week. She saw her family physician. The doctor prescribed medication and suggested she see a psychiatrist. She had the prescription filled but said she wasn't ready to see a psychiatrist.

Things calmed down in their home again for a time. The children seemed to take turns having physical illness, such as bad colds, upset stomachs, and fears at night that kept them from getting proper sleep. One of them had frightening nightmares that awakened the household when she screamed out.

The pediatrician talked at length with the mother and gave her a prescription for "nerve medicine," as she called it. Again she had the prescription filled. A state of family "cold war" developed, with little communication shared between husband and wife. Neither was able to give much attention to the children, except during serious illness or anger-provoking misbehavior. As the couple moved farther apart emotionally, each increasingly sought companionship among colleagues at work and persons with whom they became acquainted in bars and cocktail lounges. The house "went to pot." Each spent money and used charge accounts without consulting the other. Checks began to be returned from their bank marked "insufficient funds." The children were left to fend for themselves. Baby-sitters became less available as the children's behavior became less tolerable.

Eventually, she stayed away from home for two nights. The husband refused to look for her, packed clothing, and delivered the children to his mother's for care. When he returned home the third morning following her disappearance, he found her in a coma, empty pill bottles and an overturned whiskey bottle beside her. In a state of panic, he telephoned the city emergency service and she was admitted to the psychiatric ward of a nearby community hospital.

Medical measures brought her out of the coma following her overdose. The psychiatrist explained that her behavior was caused by self-destructive depression. She was placed on a treatment program that included medication and individual and group psychotherapy, plus some activity therapies. She responded well to the treatment and within two weeks was permitted home visits.

The members of the treatment team explained carefully to each of them that both her regrettable behavior and his reactions were part of the total illness picture.

"Neither of you have been yourself for some time now. The things you have done and said, the alienation between you, have all been a part of mental illness. No doubt much of what the children have done is also a part of the overall illness that has befallen your family.

"Remembering the symptoms—the drinking, the fighting, the irresponsibility, and the disappearance of love for each other within the family—is an expected thing in mental illness. Such remembering, however, is not helpful. It is a bit like remembering with hurt and angry feelings the spots of measles or the incapacity caused by a broken bone.

"So the helpful thing to do is to forget the past in this set of circumstances. That can be done as all of you remain in conversation with your counselors and therapists for a time. You can drain the natural hurt and rage that the behavior of the others has caused, not to the ones who have hurt and angered you, but to the professional helpers we have recommended to you.

"Let us help you forget the past as you concentrate on making a new beginning of a better future."

The wife continued in therapy, uncovering some of the causes of her self-destructive behaviors. She developed alternative ways of coping with them. Her husband met regularly with a group. He worked off his recollections and came to understand some of the reasons why he had not been able to respond to her more helpfully. The children talked through several "play therapy" sessions and quickly felt better. They became less upset and upsetting and their health improved.

All the members of the family learned what to do early should symptoms of mental distress appear again in any of them—get help soon!

This case demonstrates when to forget what lies behind. *Forget the past when the past consists of temporary symptoms of illness that have upset, hurt, angered, or embarrassed you and others.*

The way by which you can forget the past is also demonstrated. *Forgetting the past is made possible by telling professional helpers all the hurts, angers, confusions, and shame, fully and with feelings.*

Ultimately, of course, people may not ever really "forget" highly painful, severely hurtful, enraging events of the past. To do so would be to go beyond normal human ability. Memories do linger. From time to time the old bad feelings return. At such times, a return to one's counselor is imperative in order to redrain the unhelpful emotions that may have been stirred up anew.

It is possible, however, effectively to "forget" the past by draining and redraining those feelings to professional helpers. The New Testament was originally written in the ancient Greek language. The old Greek word that is translated "forgive" literally means "to let go." Although people cannot reasonably wipe from memory the symptoms of illness that have hurt, they can "let go" of the feelings that those tragic symptoms caused.

This is done by the "draining off" to objective professional helpers mentioned above. The way by which this draining off and letting go takes place can most readily be explained by the following story.

When I was ten years old, my father died following a brief illness caused by heart trouble. A day or two after the funeral, a group of neighborhood and church friends of my mother gathered in our home.

They helped my mother "go through" all of my father's things. Each coat, sweater, tool, book had a memory attached. My mother would look at an object and tell her memories with great emotion.

Some of the memories attached to those objects were

happy ones and as my mother told the story of the item, they would all join in laughter. Still other objects had been the source of dissatisfaction and my mother would express her indignation or resentment toward my father that she still felt when she saw those things.

Some of the memories were quite sad and my mother and the other women wept together for a time. Then they would dry their eyes and my mother would decide what to do with the item.

Some things went into the waste can, others to the Goodwill clothing drive. Still others she kept for herself, and many other things for me. Some of the things she felt my father would have wanted a certain relative or friend to have.

By the end of the day she was relaxed, naturally a little sad, but also filled with happy thoughts of their lives together. And she had gotten a lot of strong feelings drained so she could "let go" of their power. Mentally she went through this kind of procedure briefly time and again. Sometimes a song on the radio or the sight of a piece of woodwork, such as my father had made during his life, would cause her to relive and refeel the past. When that was over, she had let go some more. And the more she let go of the past, the more free she was to live fully the life still left to her.

In the same way, "forgetting" the past is done by draining the feelings; hence, letting go of the hurt, resentment, fear, pain, and shame.

There are times, however, when it is important to remember the past. The when and the how of this are presented in the next chapter.

9. Remember the Past

The Christian faith is built on remembering. Christians have received from Jewish heritage the importance of remembering. The inspiration that carried the Hebrew people throughout written history is that of remembering how God had delivered the Israelites out of the slavery of ancient Egypt and into a promised land. The faith of Israel is built on remembering, in every time of persecution and all manner of afflictions, that their God did deliver them. And because God has delivered them in the past, they live in faith that God will again.

Jesus followed this example in what Christians call the institution of the Sacrament of Holy Communion, or the Lord's Supper. Jesus took a symbolic meal of ancient times and said to his disciples, "This do in remembrance of me." Christians in every time of persecution and all manner of afflictions, as well as in times of affluence, have inspiration to continue to live in the present in love, facing the future with hope, because they remember Jesus.

Perhaps nothing in the care of the convalescent mental patient is as important as knowing when to remember the personal past. I recall talking with a convalescing patient who was overwhelmed at the prospect of the major financial crisis his sickness had caused. Not only had he been out of work for a considerable time, but the bills from hospital and doctors far exceeded the benefits of his medical insurance. On top of that, further expenses continued with inflation, school costs, overdue mortgage payments, etc.

As he was talking with increased agitation and deepening gloom about the finances, his wife interrupted and said: "Jake. We'll make it. We always do." He stopped a moment, then relaxed and said that this time it seemed different.

"I'm sure this does seem different to you. And in a way this time is different. Remember, though, the year Charlie was born? You had been on strike with your union for eleven weeks. And when I was driving to the doctor I wrecked the car. And we didn't have collision insurance, so it was a total loss. And the only thing you said then was: 'So long as you and the baby are going to be all right there is nothing else to worry about.'

"We ate food from your mother's pantry. We used the wood from the old shed you tore down for that neighbor to burn in the fireplace so we didn't use fuel oil. And I typed out bills for the doctor to help pay her off. And my brother lent us enough money to pay the interest on the mortgage so the building and loan company didn't mind our taking time to catch up with the payments. And the people at the church . . ."

"O.K., O.K., I give up," he laughed. "I know we've always

made it. This time I don't see how, but we always have, so I guess we will."

"To tell you the truth, I don't see *how* this time either, but we will," she replied. And they embraced.

One time to remember what lies behind, as demonstrated above, is when the remembering is supportive, helpful, positive, and encouraging.

Another time to remember the past is when the convalescent patient seems "locked in" to sick thoughts.

Often a convalescing mental patient will seem to become caught in a "single track" stream of thoughts. The "track" may be depressive, suspicious, fearful, angry, etc. Attempts to change the subject to some contemporary matter such as a television program, ball game, or news item may fail. The reason for failing to get the convalescing person out of the symptomatic rut is that few contemporary matters have much emotional appeal to the patient. Convalescing patients, especially those recently returned from a hospital environment, may have little feel for or interest in ball games, current politics, or a new fad. They have no feelings attached to such recent things, which may have happened while they were away—or were "out of it," as the young people say.

But memories of pleasant past experiences do have feelings attached to them. The patient does not have to reach or strain to get in touch emotionally with such events. The feelings and the interest are already there. The fact that there is already an emotional attachment enables the convalescent to slip from the "sick" preoccupation.

You may test this yourself with the following exercise: Think of some restaurant that you have heard or read about, but have never visited. You may have an idle interest. If things are going well with you, you may even have a curiosity about the place or an inclination to visit it sometime.

Now recall the best food you ever had as a child. What was it? Where did you have it? Who prepared it? A picnic that was fun? Fish you caught in a mountain stream and prepared over an open fire? Sunday dinner? The little place with the open-hearth fire where you honeymooned? Your grandmother's kitchen at Thanksgiving? The place where the other kids "hung out" with hamburgers and milkshakes? Where? When? Who?

You probably can almost smell the aroma, taste the food, hear the music of voices, brook, violins, jukebox. *Because* there are feelings attached to it, your response is more than idle interest, curiosity, or an inclination to do something "sometime." You are already there emotionally. In memory, the past comes back into the present because your feelings are already attached.

You may fear that the convalescent will be upset by memories of the past that were happy then, away from the troubles of the present. You may worry that the memory of people and places now gone will cause bittersweet nostalgia, a certain sadness, a romantic longing for that which was and perhaps can be no more.

Fear not such things. Past treasures are a part of us that even when gone can bring relief to the mind troubled by present pain. Sometimes remembering what lies behind is a part of the draining off, described in the preceding chapter. A good cry is better than fearful suspicions. For a time, a good laugh at some old family fun helps far more than concern with current crises. It also helps restore the convalescent patient to the mental energy level necessary for facing the not-so-funny present.

Finally, remembering together is a kind of sharing. Sharing the present is seldom possible when one person has been through the crisis of acute mental illness and the other person has only been able to stand outside the patient's inner world and worry and wonder. It sometimes seems odd that two persons cannot communicate very well in the here and now, but can become close and mutually supportive when they share the past. I have known a number of convalescing patients who felt complete futility in communicating with me about today, let alone tomorrow. But as soon as we go back to the past, a change comes over them. They open up emotionally, become talkative and lose their sense of despair. They begin to share.

How do you get the convalescent patient to remember what lies behind? This is *not* done by saying: "Now you stop thinking those thoughts! Switch to something else!"

Telling the convalescent patient not to be depressed, not to worry, not to be suspicious, fearful, or whatever, is a bit like getting close to the bank of a river and shouting at a drowning person, "SWIM!"

The way to help a person remember the past is to mention a specific memory. Examples are: "Remember the swing we used to like when we were kids?" "Do you remember your favorite place to be when you were a child? Mine was a treehouse." "What was the warmest room in winter at your childhood home?"

Helping patients to remember something pleasant is throwing a lifeline *to which they are already attached.* Emotionally they will pull themselves toward you and away from sickness.

Remember the past when the convalescent patient needs to be helped out of the rut of sick thought. Do it by asking or reminding of the past, not by saying, "Quit dwelling on those sick thoughts" or by trying to arouse interest in something to which there is no prior emotional attachment.

There are times when even the recollections of the past, as well as present preoccupations, seem to be confused, weird, strange nonsense. The next chapter will deal with the sense in the nonsense that is so vitally important in the care of the convalescent mental patient.

10. Discerning the Sense in Nonsense

Some convalescing mental patients seem to act or talk "nonsense" at times. This can be quite disturbing to family and friends. The "nonsense" interferes with communication. It is highly frustrating. The temptation is to "write off" the seeming nonsense with the pat solution, "She's still crazy!" or, "He's hopeless since he lost his mind." Writing off the nonsense, however, is not helpful in caring for the mental patient who has come home to convalesce.

Comprehending the "sense" in the "nonsense" is important in helping the convalescing person. One need not be highly trained in psychology to learn what a recovering patient means by speaking or acting in a "crazy" way.

My personal therapist taught me years ago that people unskilled in psychology or psychiatry often have an excellent chance of comprehending the meaning in seemingly meaningless behavior. He gave as an example an incident from his early practice with "schizophrenic" patients. One patient disturbed him considerably because he could not figure out what the patient was talking about when the patient spoke "nonsense." Finally the therapist invited another patient to sit in on a counseling session. After a few minutes of listening to "crazy talk," the doctor turned to the other patient and asked if she could tell what the patient in treatment was trying to communicate.

"Of course," replied the recovering patient. "Just look how he is sitting. He is leaning back, looking away, holding his hands over his ears part of the time. He is saying he does not want to talk with you!" The doctor then turned to the patient and asked if this was a correct interpretation. The patient sat forward, lowered his hands from his ears, and said: "Yes. I've been trying to tell you that I don't want to talk with you and you just won't understand. You are just like my father. He never understood me. He still doesn't."

Following that session, the patient and the doctor made rapid progress in communicating. The patient recovered from the acute stage of his illness quickly. This success was made possible, not because of the years of training and skill of the therapist, but because of the simple observation of an untrained recovering patient.

I recall seemingly nonsensical communication from a young woman who suffered from serious brain damage. She was so "retarded" that she could not speak. When admitted to the hospital, she uttered grunting or groaning noises at times. At other times, she squealed or made a kind of "cackling" sound. Sometimes she whimpered. She also made a lot of strange motions with her hands and arms. Occasionally, she grabbed people by the hand and stared at their fingers. Other behaviors included putting her fingers into her mouth, grimacing, gesturing wildly, pulling her ears. Most of the staff and patients at the hospital initially considered these actions to be nonsense. A few of the more experienced nurses' aides, however, felt that she was communicating to the best of her ability.

When she pulled a person's hand and stared at it, they decided she was looking to see if the person wore rings or other jewelry. One aide put this theory to a test and brought her an inexpensive "junk jewelry" ring. The patient squealed and cackled her laugh with obvious joy. The staff realized these sounds were her way of expressing happiness. They looked for other ways to comprehend the sense in the nonsense. They noted that she pulled her ears and pointed wildly at the ward television set at times. She did the same with the music therapist whenever he visited the ward. They decided she was indicating that she wanted to hear music when she pulled her ears. This proved to be correct. Whenever music was played in response to those actions, she exuded happy sounds.

As time went on, more communications were comprehended. Putting fingers to her mouth indicated she wanted to eat or drink. The grunting or whimpering sounds meant she was unhappy, needed to go to the bathroom, etc.

The chaplain was visiting the ward one day and another patient said, "Reverend, she wants you to read the Bible." The chaplain glanced at the girl and saw that she was staring at the palms of her hands. She was holding them in front of her as one might hold a book. The chaplain then read briefly from the Bible to her. The words may or may not have meant anything to her, but she knew what kind of attention this particular chaplain seemed to pay to patients. He read the Bible to those who asked him to. She was asking for some of his attention in the only way she could.

All of the above demonstrates a way by which one can comprehend sense in the nonsense of convalescent mental patients. Listen to the words, notice the actions, and then ask a recovering patient what you think she or he might be communicating. One convalescent patient was able to talk quite rationally with family and friends much of the time. Occasionally, however, he would suddenly begin to laugh "inappropriately" while the family were talking. When asked why the laughter, his response was to stop laughing and gaze at the floor, saying nothing. He withdrew emotionally from the family at such times and would sulk in silence for several hours or the rest of the day. Sometimes he would leave the room to be by himself.

This was naturally irritating and frustrating to the family. They consulted the patient's social worker. The social worker suggested that the family notice what was being talked about, how long the conversation had been going on, who was speaking, etc., when the convalescent patient began the "crazy laughter." The family followed this advice. They discovered that so long as the family members were having friendly conversation, the patient "acted normally." However, as soon as some disagreement or argument began to develop, the laughter commenced. They decided that the convalescent patient was comfortable with friendly "small talk" but became upset when strong feelings emerged.

When he was a young child, his parents frequently had bitter quarrels and sometimes fought physically. This was frightening and upsetting to him. On several occasions, he had tried to get them to stop the fighting and both parents had "turned against him" and punished him for "interfering." He had felt that he should never try to stop people from arguing or fighting again, because he had been punished for doing so in his childhood. When he was older, he still experienced the fear and upset from childhood whenever people disagreed or raised their voices in argument. But he was unable rationally to say, "You stop fighting, because that scares me." He did "learn" during the acute phase of his illness that when he began to laugh out loud, people stopped whatever they were doing and did not punish him. They simply became confused. His way of stopping family arguments *and* avoiding punishment was to laugh "inappropriately."

He still was afraid and felt guilty for "interfering," however, and withdrew from the family. As the family realized this with the help of the social worker, they talked with him about his behavior. They encouraged him to go ahead and laugh when he felt the fear coming on. They assured him they would not punish him. The family also told him they would not stop disagreeing with each other to be sure he was comfortable all of the time. Before many weeks had passed, he stopped the laughter when disagreements arose. He simply left the room so the rest of the family could "argue in peace." Later he even began to announce, "I'd better leave while you folks fuss." In time he was able to tolerate family discord and as his therapy concluded he began to give his opinions during arguments, thus recovering the ability to relate in a more fully human way.

To comprehend the sense in the nonsense of convalescing mental patients, notice not so much what is said or done but *when* the nonsense occurs. Families should talk with trained counselors about what is going on when strange behavior occurs. Untrained persons should not attempt to "analyze" the symbolic meaning of actions and words that do not make sense without the help of experts. Interpretations of behavior should be "checked out" with the recovering patient carefully and diplomatically.

Open-ended interpretations are more helpful than dogmatic "closed" opinions. For example, in the situation of the laughing young man described above, a dogmatic, closed interpretation from a family member might sound as follows:

"I know why you laugh that crazy laugh. It's because you are mad at us for some reason. Admit it! Tell us why you are angry with us. We'll settle this nonsense once and for all!"

Obviously such an accusing, authoritarian approach will increase the anxiety, fear, or anger of the convalescent patient. The patient already has great discomfort with the idea of "interfering" with the family, and will be increasingly afraid if "accused" of being angry.

An open-ended comment that, in this instance, proved helpful was: "I talked with your social worker the other day and we discussed the way you laugh at times, as you are doing now. We wondered what the laughter might mean. We thought it might mean that you are getting uncomfortable with our having this argument. You might wish we would stop. Then again, the laughter could mean something else. Maybe it is your way of letting us know that you are getting bored with the conversation, but are too polite to let us know that so you can leave the room. Or there may be other reasons. We don't have to know all of them or any of them. If you are willing to continue to laugh when you feel the urge, we'll not be angry with you. We know you are communicating to us. If you will be patient, we will understand in time. It is all right for you to laugh or leave. We get frustrated by that, but then you probably get frustrated with us at times too."

In the above, the recovering patient is not forced into a corner. The way is left open for the continuation of the odd behavior, *and* for more direct communication when the patient is emotionally ready. When both options are left open, recovering patients usually move toward more direct communication.

Offering alternative interpretations is also more productive than making single-idea statements. "You may be uncomfortable . . . bored . . . irritated . . . , etc.," gives opportunity for the convalescent patient to consider various meanings of behavior which may be as incomprehensible to him or her as it is to others.

11. Don't Keep Secrets

Protecting convalescent mental patients is a major concern to those caring for them. "For their own good" is a slogan that summarizes the attitude people have for much of what they do in relation to recovering patients.

Such protection, "for their own good," however excellent the intention, is often contrary to the best interest of the patient. Among the most frequent examples of this well-meant but sometimes sabotaging behavior is keeping secrets from the patient.

By keeping secrets, I mean withholding from the patient information or opinions or feelings which family and friends fear the patient might not be able to handle without getting upset. At first glance, this protective attitude seems good. Much of the time it is not.

The reason that keeping things from the convalescent patient is not generally helpful is based on one fact: great self-doubt or lack of confidence is common to recovering patients. Most persons recuperating from any illness need their self-confidence increased. When information or feelings are withheld, the unintended message that patients receive is that others doubt them also.

Sooner or later, patients learn about information or opinions not shared with them. They then realize they have been excluded. They begin to wonder what else is being withheld. If they question others, they know they are sounding suspicious. People will think they are getting "paranoid." If they do not question, they cannot be sure what all is going on "behind their backs." Doubt and distrust in self and others increases.

Therefore, share things diplomatically but openly with convalescent patients. Do not whisper conversations about them. Say what you have to say to them in front of them. Do not ask helping professionals to keep your conversations with them secret from the patient. Trust between patient and doctor, social worker, nurse, teacher, chaplain, etc., is damaged if the professional helper has conversations or makes plans with others "behind the patient's back." In my experience of over twenty years, patients almost always learn of such covert behavior. They then suffer a setback more severe than open confrontations may cause.

Increasingly, laws are being passed granting patients "the right to know" what is being planned for them. The result has been a more rapid improvement in patients than in the "old days" when the patient was "the last to know."

As stated above, information is withheld from patients in fear that it will upset the patient. The information may indeed upset the patient briefly, but at least the patient knows what is happening. To be kept "in the dark" is seldom beneficial in the long run for the patient.

Along with protective attitudes toward patients, there may be a second reason why people keep things from them. The second reason is that those who are keeping secrets are themselves upset by the concealed matters. With the excuse that they are protecting the patients, they also protect themselves from upsetting conversations. The following is a typical example.

The father of a large family called the family together shortly before one of the grown children was to be discharged from a mental hospital.

"Now we all know," he said, "that Joanna has been through a lot in recent weeks. She is coming home from the hospital for the weekend. She does not know that her brother Timmy is separated from his wife and talking about getting a divorce.

"I do not think we should let Joanna know about that. She has always been close to Timmy and his wife. If she learns they are talking about divorce, it will only upset her. It may cause a relapse. We don't want that. We want the best for Joanna.

"Besides, I don't think Timmy is serious about this divorce business at all. I think they are just having some typical marriage difficulties. Instead of going on with things and patching them up the way your mother and I have always done, they are into this divorce talk. Well, that is just a passing phase. They don't mean it. It is all a 'tempest in a teapot,' if you ask me. So why upset Joanna by talking about it at all? It isn't going to happen, so I don't want to hear any more about it. Right?"

In the above statement the father is saying two things. One, he wishes to give Joanna a smooth chance to recover. Second, he obviously has emotional problems of his own with the thought that there might be a divorce in the family. So he asks the family not to talk about it at all "to protect Joanna from being upset." Actually he is also upset by thought or talk of the divorce and is protecting himself, as well as the convalescent Joanna.

It is probable that Joanna will sooner or later learn that Timmy and his wife are separated whether divorce takes place or not. Then she will feel that the family doubted her ability to handle the information. She will feel excluded by them. She will also have increased apprehensions about her own competence to cope with the negative factors in family life.

Joanna may have already suspected that things were not well with Timmy and his wife, especially if she *has* been close to them. Also, the probability is that she will be able to handle the information reasonably if she is "in on it" from the start.

Naturally, it is important to *time* wisely the sharing of possibly upsetting information. For example, in the situation outlined above, it would not be wise for the family to greet Joanna at the gate of the hospital with statements such as:

"Oh, Joanna we're glad you are getting to come home, but, my God, such an awful thing is going on. Timmy and his wife are divorcing. But don't get upset by that, horrible as it is."

A more helpful approach is to give the recovering patient

time to get readjusted and settled, and the family time to get used to having the patient back. Then a statement such as the one following may be appropriate:

"Wow, that *was* a good meal despite the fact that we're probably all a little nervous. We don't want to do or say anything upsetting. I'm sure you are not as comfortable as you will be, Joanna. You've been used to the hospital routine and so on and you may feel a little unsure these first hours and days home.

"You may have noticed that some of us are a bit on edge. Well, it is not because of your coming home. We're glad you're here. That helps.

"But, you see, there is another problem. Well, not problem maybe, but concern. I'm not sure if you want to hear about it just yet. It can wait if you need more time. It isn't life or death or anything like that, but we are concerned."

The patient will almost always reply with something such as: "Gosh, Dad, don't keep me in suspense any longer. What is it? The oil crisis, or the dog is going to have pups, or *what?*"

"It is about Timmy and his wife, I'm afraid. I don't like to think about it, but, well, you know, or maybe you don't know—I didn't have the faintest notion and I still refuse to believe it is serious—but Timmy has moved out of the house. They have separated, at least temporarily."

At this point the patient should be given a chance to assimilate the information and respond. The patient may respond by saying:

"It's about time Timmy came to his senses. That little

tramp has had him hoodwinked far too long!" or: "Oh, crud! Everything and everybody is falling apart. Maybe they ought to talk with my doctor before they really do something they'll regret for a long time." Or: "I don't want to hear about it. That's a lie. I want to eat some more supper." Or: "All mimzy were the loots and floots." Or: "Poor Timmy. I'm so sorry. For both of them really. Tell me all about it. Are they going to get a divorce? I'm sorry, but I want to know what's going on. I'm upset naturally, but tell me. I need to know." Or: "I'm glad I'm not the only one screwed up in this family."

The response of the convalescent patient will clue the family as to how to proceed. Mental patients may be better equipped emotionally to handle upsetting situations than family or friends who have not had the benefit of recent psychiatric treatment programs.

Convalescent mental patients have a lot to teach family and friends about how to cope. After all, they have "been to the bottom," in a sense. They have faced the worst and overcome it, or are in the process of overcoming it. Others who have remained the "outsane" may not have the renewal and restoration of body, mind, and spirit that recovering patients have.

People will never learn more effective ways of coping with difficulties and decisions of life so long as they keep secrets from convalescent patients. Convalescent patients will never feel they are "back again" until they have been allowed to share in all of life—the good and the bad.

This chapter would not be complete without a few paragraphs about the "exception to the rule" in regard to keeping secrets from convalescent patients. There are a few instances when delaying the giving of information *is* in the best interest of the convalescent patient. Usually the qualified professional helper will know when these circumstances are present and will advise the family accordingly.

Consider the following situation: A seventy-nine-year-old woman suffered from organic brain disease caused by infection when she was quite young. For fifteen years she had become increasingly dependent on her sister, who was two years younger than she. The sister was a very motherly person who often did things for the patient that the patient could have done for herself. For example, she told the patient (who lived in the sister's home) that she should not try to walk to the dinner table. The sister, instead, insisted that the patient remain in bed or sitting in her wheelchair, since the patient was "unsteady" when walking. The patient got to the point that she felt totally unable to care for herself, even to remain alone in the house while the sister went for groceries.

The family cooperated by providing "sitter service" whenever the sister was to be out of the house. There was no medical reason for the patient to be so overly cared for.

A series of upsetting events took place in the family. One grandson had minor troubles with the law. A niece and her husband divorced after twenty-three years of marriage. A granddaughter and her husband were expecting their first child before the husband had completed his college work. And then the sister became ill and died suddenly.

The patient became hysterical, extremely anxious. She

refused to stay in the house and demanded to be taken to the hospital in which her sister had died. The patient was in good physical health and was discharged from the hospital. She begged to be placed in some kind of institution, vowing never to return to the house. Her pension was not sufficient for her to be placed in a nursing home without support from the family. She swallowed a number of aspirin tablets and cut her wrists in suicidal attempts. She fought with nursing personnel.

Medication was prescribed and the patient was admitted from the hospital to a nursing home. She gradually began to recover. During this time her favorite niece and the husband were having marital problems after twenty-five years of marriage. The patient made good progress in her convalescence, relearned to do things for herself in the nursing home. She no longer needed a wheelchair. She began to get interested in activities and the nursing home staff.

The family decided they would not share the latest marriage crisis with her, feeling this would be one more "straw on the camel's back." They were advised that in time the patient would be able emotionally to handle further misfortunes and upsets of life, but that for the time being, she should not have one more added worry.

This example demonstrates that there *are* times when it is in the patient's interest to postpone information that might be upsetting. Most of the time, however, patients have a legal and moral right to know the truth especially as it affects them. Keeping secrets does not foster trust and confidence. Therefore, almost always, with a wise sense of timing, share with the convalescent patient. Do not keep secrets.

Inevitably, when people care for the convalescent mental patient, mistakes will be made. The next chapter is a guide for those times when you have made a mistake.

12. When You Have Made a Mistake

When you have made a mistake in anything, there are three possible responses. One is to dismiss the mistake from mind, pretend it didn't happen, ignore it. A second is to plunge into the agony of despair, feel terribly guilty, lose sleep, brood. A third is to recognize and admit the mistake and make whatever restitution is possible.

For various reasons most people react to different kinds of mistakes in specific ways. For example, one person may "laugh off" forgetting an appointment, yet be unreasonably upset over a mistake in the checking account. Another person may respond to being overdrawn at the bank with a shrug. That person, however, may become painfully embarrassed and weep over having momentarily forgotten an appointment or someone's name. There are people who respond to *all* kinds of mistakes in one of the three ways suggested above.

When it comes to the care of the convalescent mental patient, however, mistakes seem more serious. This is because people feel that "the stakes are much higher." Therefore, they react more strongly when they feel they have made a mistake in the care of the recovering patient.

For example, when family members have done or said something that seems to have caused the patient to regress, they may become upset and overreact. They may not just dismiss the incident, but actually deny that it ever happened. Or they may go into spasms of remorse and agonize terribly, feeling that something has taken place that could never be undone.

Obviously such extreme reactions are not so constructive as the third response suggested above—that of calmly recognizing and admitting the mistake and making amends. This is not as easy as it sounds in the emotionally tense atmosphere that people feel when relating to the convalescent patient. Therefore, several things are important in acquiring the ability to handle mistakes helpfully with recovering patients.

The first step in working toward a happy resolution when a mistake has been made is to realize that mistakes with convalescent mental patients are no different from any other mistakes in human life. Most mistakes can be corrected. Saying or doing the "wrong" thing in relating to a convalescent patient can be made right, just as saying or doing the wrong thing with any other person can be amended.

The reason this is true is that mental patients are *people*, just like other people. There may be times when *they* feel "different," "one of a kind," or not normal. Others may think they are different, "not normal."

All people at times feel different. All people seem to others to be abnormal at times. I recall the events surrounding a severe tornado that swept through our city causing almost total property destruction in an area one quarter of a mile wide and ten miles long. Miraculously there were only five deaths among the population of a hundred thousand who lived and worked in that area.

One of the feelings that seemed most unchristian to me was a sense of relief, almost of celebration, when I learned that none of *my* family or friends had been killed. I have heard such feelings reported by military personnel, when, after a battle, they inwardly rejoiced that they had been neither killed nor seriously wounded. They felt guilt at being happy to be alive when so many others had died. Nevertheless, I felt estranged from others because of my inward glee at surviving. I did not want others to know of my pleasure when there was so much possible pain and death around.

Later in the evening as neighbors gathered in the remains of the house we lived in, they reported the same pleasure and accompanying feeling of being "different" because they were in a mood to celebrate in the midst of all that rubble. We discovered that, although we felt different, not normal, we were very much alike. And so, by candlelight (for all power was shut off for days following) we had a "block party" and celebrated in a festive mood. We consumed all the food and drink on hand because we knew it would all spoil anyway. At the same time, we listened to reports of the great tragedy on a transistor radio. Each of us had felt not normal in responding to calamity with cheerful abandon. Yet that turned out to be the way the whole neighborhood felt. We must have looked weird to others as we laughed, drank, ate, sang, told jokes while rescue helicopters circled above and sirens of fire truck and ambulance sounded continuously against a background of chain saws and bulldozers.

The same kind of thing is true with recovering mental patients. They may feel abnormal because of their experiences with despair, suspicion, immobility, overactivity, apathy, etc. Yet their range of feelings and behavior is a part of being genuine human beings. As the apostle Paul once wrote, "No temptation has overtaken you that is not common to people" (I Cor. 10:13). "Mentally ill human beings are more human than otherwise," someone has said. Therefore, to make a mistake in the care of the convalescent mental patient is no different from making any other kind of mistake.

When you have made a mistake in caring for a mental patient, realize that the mistake is correctable. Accept it, admit it, and make any restitution necessary.

Ignoring the mistake, acting as if it had not taken place, is unhelpful. Agonized brooding and self-condemnation regarding a mistake is counterproductive. Admitting, apologizing, and offering to "make up" for the mistake almost always results in continued improvement of the convalescent patient. It also increases comfortable communication among family, friends, and the patient.

A most common example of "mistakes" made in relation to recovering mental patients is that of not taking the patient seriously. I recall an instance told to me by a psychiatrist. The doctor had received a telephone call from a patient discharged from the hospital. The patient, a middle-aged man, had a schedule of outpatient appointments to see a counselor. The man telephoned the doctor one evening and said he was getting depressed again. He was afraid he would commit suicide.

"Now, do not get carried away. Setbacks are to be expected," the doctor told the patient over the telephone. "I am just about to leave for a long weekend of fishing. You should forget your troubles and try to have a little time for pleasure yourself. Follow my example."

"But, doctor, I don't think I can. I have been saving my medicine and am tempted to take it all at once," the patient replied.

"Nonsense. You are better. Now you just forget those pills and keep the appointment with your counselor next week. Try to have a relaxed weekend. Good-by."

The doctor enjoyed the long weekend but returned the following Monday morning to learn that the patient was in a coma in the intensive care unit of the local general hospital. The patient had taken an overdose of medication, been rushed to the hospital by the family, but was now expected to survive. The doctor was notified the moment the patient recovered consciousness.

"I goofed. I made a mistake and it almost cost you your life," the doctor said when first speaking to the recovering patient. "I won't do that again, ever."

"Oh, that's all right, Doc. I think I goofed too. I should have gone to the hospital myself despite what you said. From now on we'll both take me more seriously when I get that way. But I don't think I will again. It was too risky."

In the aftermath of this incident the family very much wanted the patient to change doctors. But the patient did not, because, as the patient put it: "That doctor is not afraid to admit to making mistakes. That I like and trust."

Had the doctor ignored the mistake or been so embarrassed professionally as not to be able to function effectively any longer, no one would have benefited. As it turned out, all concerned learned something vital.

It is hoped that all who read this will also gain from the mistake of that doctor. Always take the recovering patient seriously. It may be a matter of life and death. And always admit and make amends when a mistake has been made.

13. Facing the Threat of Relapse

Mental patients who have come home and the persons who care for them share the fear of a total collapse of the patient back into acute mental illness. Professional helpers, whether we like to admit it or not, also have this fear lurking around the corners of our minds. When we know what to do and how to do it if total relapse should occur, the fears subside considerably.

A relapse usually takes the form of a return of the symptoms that initially caused the patient's admission to a psychiatric facility. These may include the total immobility of the patient, staying in bed, neither noticing nor responding to others. The patient may sleep or seem to sleep, or just sit or lie vacantly staring. Another form of total collapse may be an explosion of activity with possible combative attempts to hurt others, destroy property, etc. Yet another form of regression to acute sickness may be an extreme acting out of highly suspicious attitudes. In this instance, the patients may barricade themselves in rooms or houses, threatening violence to any who approach.

The more common relapse, however, is that of patients who begin to talk and behave in inappropriate ways, not just at certain times, but all the time. They may not respond to the presence of others, but may jabber nonsense "word salads," may posture and gesture oddly, whether anyone is near them or not. Or they may seem relatively "normal" until spoken to. Then their response is nonsensical in behavior or speech or both.

In instances of complete collapse the family should communicate with the appropriate helping professionals as soon as possible. They will need to know whether the patient has stopped taking medication, has been drinking or taking other drugs. Advice is needed to ensure that patients not harm themselves or others.

It is also important for family and friends to realize that the return to acute illness does not mean that the patient will remain that way forever. Such recurrences are almost always temporary. Relapses should be reviewed in the same way one considers the instance of a reformed alcoholic "falling off the wagon" once in a while. Long periods of recovery in many illnesses are interrupted by temporary setbacks. Such relapses should not be considered as a final doom—that convalescent patients have "lost" their minds eternally.

Medication may need to be readjusted. Various other medical procedures may need to be repeated or "stepped up," as in the case of patients receiving "maintenance" dialysis treatments. The recovering patient may need to be rehospitalized briefly. Or the patient may simply need the reassurance that if help is needed, it will be increased.

A number of convalescent patients want the reassurance that they could return to the security of the hospital environment should they ever need it. A temporary flare-up of acute symptoms treated promptly with professional collaboration may give this needed reassurance. In the late 1950's the new psychotropic medications became available. This enabled many long-term state hospital patients to return to the larger community. A curious thing happened. Patients who were given increasingly longer home visits with decreasingly frequent returns to the hospital for a checkup did quite well. But when the hospital personnel finally told the patients that they were now cured and did not have to come back for any more follow-up visits, many patients promptly regressed into acute mental illness.

The cause for this was simply stated by one patient. After she had been back in the hospital for three days her acute illness cleared almost completely. When asked what had happened, she said: "Well, when they told me I didn't have to come back again, I thought the hospital wouldn't ever help me again. I felt abandoned."

Most patients need the assurance that should they ever need further psychiatric help, they will get it quickly. But there is another kind of assurance the patient may be asking for.

Some patients feel that they are welcome back with the family so long as they continue to improve but that they would be rejected should their illness return. These recovering patients may need to "test" the family to see if the family will stick with them "through thick and thin." In these cases, professional helpers may decide that it would be most helpful for the recovering patient to stay out of the hospital. This assurance from family and the professionals, that patients will not be abandoned should they suffer a temporary relapse, often results in a rapid recovery outside the hospital setting.

At still other times the collapse into illness may be the way that patients let the family know they are not going to be comfortable staying home. The patients may not want to go back to the hospital—they may want to be more independent. Again, professional consultation is important to determine whether this is the message the patient is giving. If it is, relocation of the patient to a "halfway house" or other living place in the community will resolve the problem of recurring acute illness.

I am thinking of a man in his late forties. He was a long-term patient in a state hospital. Medications and newer forms of therapy proved that he was not "chronic" or incurable. He cleared from his "crazy" symptoms of many years. He became active in hospital community events. His high intelligence had long been covered over by the symptoms of illness. He became so "normal" that he was allowed to return to his family. In a short time he became sick again. He cleared almost immediately upon his return to the hospital and was returned home shortly. The same thing happened again. And again.

Finally the decision was made to allow him to leave the hospital, not to return home, but to move in with an elderly couple. The couple's children were all living far away from them. They desired someone to live in their spare bedroom and help with household chores in exchange for room and board. The recovering patient was able to live with them without another mental collapse. He completed college work that had been interrupted many years before and continued to live with the elderly couple happily after securing a job in the community.

This last story demonstrates what may be the most difficult task for those who love and want to care for a convalescent mental patient—that of letting go when to do so is in the best interest of the patient. To allow a recovering patient, or anyone you love, to leave, go his or her own way, is painful. This is true when children marry and move away from home. It is also true when one's child enlists in the military service. And it is true in divorce situations.

To paraphrase a popular song, "If you love me, let me know by letting me go." This indeed is an anguishing aspect of expressing love and care for some people.

When a convalescent mental patient reverts to acute illness, make sure he or she inflicts no harm to self or others. Communicate with professional helpers. Cooperate in providing the assurance the patient may seek—whether it be to return to the hospital or to "weather the storm" at home. And if what is needed by the patient is independence, if you love the person, let the person go. Turn to your own counselors for help in any of these situations.

14. Preventing Suicide and Homicide

Two things cannot be changed. Suicide and homicide cannot be corrected, changed, or called back. Almost everything else can be turned around or brought back. Financial problems can be resolved through refinancing, budget revision, legal bankruptcy. Health problems can be alleviated. Even such dreaded ailments as heart disease and cancer can be brought into remission, if not outright cure. Divorced people can remarry. The mentally retarded are trainable, if not "educable." Wars end. The broken can be bound up, mended, repaired. But death is permanent and unchangeable.

There are exceptions to the above dogmatic statement. My daughter is an emergency duty nurse in a large city hospital. On almost every evening shift when she is on duty someone is brought to the emergency room seemingly D.O.A., i.e., "dead on arrival." Yet many of these patients are revived by procedures of modern medical science. Such procedures are referred to by various phrases. In our city's most prestigious hospital the term "Code" is used. In suburban hospitals a number is added, so that the public-address system echoes with "Code 300 in the E.R." In the public hospital for the indigent ill, they simply refer to "a room 9." Regardless of the language used, the point is that highly trained, equipped, and disciplined medical-nursing personnel respond within seconds and often the dead are literally brought back to life.

The purpose of this chapter, however, is not to extol what was once considered a mysterious and magical miracle and has now become a routine medical procedure. The purpose, rather, is to indicate what you can do to prevent suicide and murder which, despite modern medicine, may be a permanent and unchangeable circumstance.

I will not cite statistics indicating how widespread suicide is, nor how seldom mental patients resort to homicide. Suicide is a major cause of death in this country. Murder ranks farther down the list. What one needs to know is what do to about suicide and murder.

The first thing you must realize is that both suicide and murder are 95 percent preventable. To prevent suicide or murder the following should be accepted:

1. People who contemplate suicide or murder should *always* be taken seriously. There are popular rumors that people who talk about or threaten either are just seeking attention and would never do such things. Probably in 85 percent of the cases, this is true. The trouble is that one never knows when the speaker is in the 85 percent or in the 15 percent. Therefore, all suicidal talk or murderous threats should be taken seriously.

This does not mean that everyone who talks suicide or homicide will attempt it. Indeed much of the talk is a ventilation of feeling that does little harm. Still, since one never knows for sure, it is always better to be "safe than sorry."

2. Contact the professional helper of the recovering patient when threats are uttered. Follow professional advice. Qualified professionals may make mistakes, but ordinarily they have a more objective, less emotionally involved attitude toward the convalescent patient than family or friends do. There are a number of professional helpers in the mental health field who have never lost a life so long as they were kept informed about changes in the attitude of patients.

3. Take precautions to see that lethal weapons are not readily available. Do not keep guns and ammunition in unlocked places. When people seem to be in a destructive mood, do not let them drive automobiles, ride motorcycles, etc. Keep track of pills and household poisons. Do not assume that such things will keep count of themselves. Since so much violence is enacted by persons who are intoxicated, do not allow convalescent patients to get drunk.

4. Avoid severe confrontations with enraged persons. Do not be authoritarian. Don't back a person into a corner either physically or emotionally. Convalescent mental patients need time, space, and distance from others in order to rethink things. Browbeating and threatening seldom help. If force seems to be the only alternative, turn to professional help. If necessary, enlist the services of professional peace officers such as the sheriff's department or the police.

5. Do not leave deeply depressed persons alone. Few persons take their own lives when in the company of others. Should a person who is contemplating suicide, talking about

it, or leaving notes to that effect desire to take a walk or go for a drive, go along. You need not engage in conversation, nor require that the suicidal person talk to you. Just be sure the person is not alone.

6. Pay careful attention to the things convalescent patients do that may indicate they are considering suicide. Although most people give obvious and ample warning when they are moving toward life-taking actions, some signal their intentions in "code." Statements such as, "Well, pretty soon nobody will have to worry about me," or, "Before long that landlord won't be causing anybody trouble anymore," may be veiled hints that the person is planning suicide or homicide. Behavior also may indicate that the patient is serious about taking life. For example, planning for one's death by cleaning out closets, giving away long-cherished possessions, hoarding pills or poisons, stocking up on ammunition and guns, may show that the recovering patient is slipping toward a destructive course.

Talk with the patient calmly but firmly, telling of your apprehensions as to what the veiled statement or behaviors might mean. Secure the patient's cooperation in reporting such matters to the therapist. When the patient refuses, you should take the initiative in contacting the therapist yourself for advice.

7. Get the recovering patient to promise not to do anything drastic without talking the matter over with you or the helping professional. Almost always convalescent patients will keep such promises.

There are situations in which the long-term benefit of

convalescent patients requires that they move out into the world "on their own." In those circumstances, family or friends are placed in a bind when suicidal or homicidal signals are detected. To keep these persons with them at all times undermines the long-range plan. To let them be alone in their apartment when they are suicidal runs the risk of losing them. A middle-of-the-road strategy is necessary.

Say something to the convalescent patient such as: "I know you have been doing well in your apartment and that the doctor is pleased that you are making it. This week, however, you seem to be more depressed and I'm worried about you. I want you to promise to telephone me tonight around nine o'clock so I'll know how things are going. Promise to do that, please?"

The convalescent patient will appreciate both the concern and the trust, and will tend to make the phone call. At that time, a further promise can be made for another call in the morning. This gives the convalescent something to live for "until." When persons are getting deeply into suicidal or homicidal urges, they may not be able to make a promise in good conscience "never" to do something or "always" to do something. They *can* keep a promise of shorter duration. Added assurance and trust is communicated by letting convalescent patients know that they can call earlier or more often if need be. I usually summarize such an agreement with a patient by saying: "Well, we are agreed that you will telephone me between nine and ten o'clock tonight. If you need to call earlier, do so." Not long ago, I did receive an earlier call from a patient who said he could not wait until nine o'clock because he would kill himself before that hour. He said he wanted to get back to the hospital as soon as possible. He readmitted himself to the hospital and lives today to tell the story.

These are a few of the things you need to know about preventing suicide and homicide. There are rare instances, however, when, despite all efforts, people do kill. The next chapter will give ways to cope when the uncorrectable permanent decision is acted upon.

15. Coping with Suicide and Homicide

I am tempted to begin this chapter with the simple sentence, "Don't be ashamed." To do so would be reasonable and logical, for in our imperfect life and with our imperfect knowledge, tragedy does happen. When all efforts fail in the end and someone does kill self or others, the reasonable attitude is to regret but not to be ashamed.

Nobody is perfect—not convalescent mental patients, not their families, friends, nor even professional helpers. Therefore, it is logical to dismiss even so terrible a thing as suicide or murder as a part of the way things really are and have no shame, no sense of blame, no embarrassment, and no more severe aftershock than when an elderly person passes away quietly of "old age."

But life is not always logical and there are times when reason does not prevail for the genuine human being. Therefore, instead of giving such an overly simple statement, no matter how logical and reasonable it is, I give the following suggestions when the unchangeable action of suicide or murder takes place:

104

1. Although violent death is a shocking, numbing, bewildering event, one must prepare for it and have an idea of whom to contact, of what to do. Usually the police or the sheriff's office must be called. A doctor needs to be notified, especially if the doctor has been treating the victim or the perpetrator of a killing. The minister, rabbi, or priest may often be helpful. An attorney is important in any homicide case. Family and friends must be notified. When violent death takes place, as soon as you are able, *get help*. The more help the better. All the help possible is needed. Get help before doing anything else.

2. In the early hours following a violent death, accept wise advice from professionals, from people not directly involved emotionally. If someone close to you has taken his or her own life, or the life of another, you cannot be expected to think clearly for a time. The emotional shock is too great. You need others to care for you and help make difficult decisions. There will be time for you to "collect yourself" later.

3. As time passes, you will be flooded with strong emotions once the numbness has lifted. Do not fight the emotions. Share them with those who are trained and skilled in working with such situations. The emotions will run the full range. You will experience fear, sorrow, and anger. Strangely, you may feel a kind of relief that the nightmare is somehow over, the uncertainty has passed. You will know that further nightmare experiences may come, but at least something has happened that is final.

Share as many of these feelings as you can. There will be guilt and shame, not just over the death, but over your own mixed feelings about the death. You will think back and examine all the ways by which you might have prevented what happened. At other times you decide that nobody could have stopped the inevitable, that it was destined to be. For brief periods, you may find yourself doing routine things as if nothing had happened. Again you may have impulses to act differently than you ever have, to do things you never would have thought of doing a short time before. Your habits may change. You will suspect that you too are "losing" *your* mind. You may be tempted to take your own life or to commit murder yourself.

Any and all of the above may be your experience. Talking with professional helpers will assist you in the task of absorbing what has happened. With their help you can, in time, reorder your thoughts and feelings. Eventually, you can become free from the grip of severe tragedy. You can begin to live again.

4. In the aftermath of a homicide, if it was committed by a convalescent mental patient, which is extremely rare, there are two essentials. One is to come to terms with your own feelings about *what has happened* through the process of sharing described above. A second is to work out your feelings and attitudes toward the *patient*. Usually these will be mixed, as I have stated. You will probably be afraid of the patient, feel sadness for the patient, be enraged with the patient, and may feel relief that now she or he will be "off your hands" for good. You may even feel glad as you realize that now the courts and prison systems will pick up the burden of caring for the patient.

All these feelings will be intermixed. Some will be felt more strongly than others. You may feel that you never want to see or communicate with the patient again. On the other hand, you may feel great guilt, as though you were responsible. You may want to rush to the patient. You may be angry should police or other officials restrict visitation. You may feel that *you*, not the patient, should be the one arrested, tested, possibly tried, perhaps convicted.

This may be true especially when your own feelings toward the victim of the homicide were mixed or outright hostile. This latter feeling was expressed by the older brother of an eighteen-year-old convalescent who had shot their father to death. The brother said:

"The way the old man drank and beat up on mom and the rest of us, one of us should have been man enough to do that long ago. We should not have left it up to a sick kid who was too confused to realize what he was doing. We're all guilty They gotta go easy on the kid!"

Regardless of the mixed feelings following the confusion of a homicide, you will need to decide what to do in relation to the accused. Given time and opportunity to work through, to "let go," the most severe aftershock feelings, you will probably want to visit with the patient.

Authorities and medical personnel may suggest that you send word of your thoughts through detectives, attorney, nursing staff, or custody officials at first. The patient should be consulted as to whether or not he or she is "ready" to see you. Often the patient, suffering also from aftershock, is not emotionally able to see family, friends, or anyone well known to him or her. This will pass as the patient has opportunity to get over the crucial phase following a violent act.

When the time is appropriate for you to visit the patient, you will be nervous and not sure what to expect. Quite often the worst fears are groundless. There is no emotional upheaval. Almost always the reunion is calmly moving, but not emotionally upsetting to either patient or family. When proper preparation is made for the reunion, even in a jail or locked maximum-security hospital unit, it will be rewarding.

You may find the patient depressed, confused, or seeming to have forgotten the shocking episode. Sometimes the patient will be highly suspicious, claiming that he or she was "framed," or that the victim was an alien in disguise.

Usually, however, there is an expression of mild regret or mild surprise that such a thing happened, but generally there is apathy or seeming indifference about the matter. This is one of the ways by which the human mind copes with shattering experience—closing off the strong feeling so the person can continue to live without continuous torment.

One woman had been on a home visit during which she killed her spouse. Her statement is typical. She calmly said: "Well, it was a shame, but I told him I needed to go back to the hospital and he wouldn't listen. He'd be alive today if he had. But, that's past. I wonder what the judge will do about me."

Once in a while a family will stay away from the rehospitalized patient for a long time. I recall the visit of such a family to one of their members who had killed an uncle. They had neither written, telephoned, nor visited the patient for fifteen years following the death. At the urging of a dedicated young social worker and with the help of the hospital chaplain, a visit was arranged. Both family and patient were prepared for the reunion.

After a few moments of initial nervousness, the long-separated relatives greeted and embraced the patient. What had been originally planned as a brief "get reacquainted" visit quickly turned into a picnic on the campus of the hospital that lasted a full afternoon. The family revisited often and were able to persuade the authorities in their home county to drop all charges since the patient's illness had long since "run its course." The patient went home again and has lived and worked on the family farm for a number of happy years at this writing.

The point is that even in the most extreme, permanent situations there can be a rekindling of loving relationships temporarily extinguished.

5. Religious faith is a help in the restoration of relationships after terribly separating events, such as homicide. As the most critical time of the crisis of suicide or homicide passes, seek the renewal or deepening of religious faith. Often faith seems to "go out the window" when ultimate earthly tragedy enters the doorway of our lives. It is not easy to recover religious faith that has been so readily shattered by stark disaster. The help of wise, not fanatical, religious leaders and friends is usually necessary. Usually we meet God only through other people— not by reading about God.

The religious faith you deepen must include room for all the "dangers and difficulties of this mortal life." It cannot be a shallow, cheap collection of religious-sounding phrases that do not take seriously the massive impact of life and death. It must be a faith that goes beyond what you do or do not do in the care of the convalescent mental patient. It must go beyond suicide or homicide, beyond anything that science or commonsense can tell you about the infinite and the eternal.

Such faith will not explain away all mysteries, solve all problems, or undo from heavenly sources what has been permanently done on earth. Such faith will, however, give guidance as to the next steps you are to take, and will help you know and feel that *"nothing* shall separate" you from God.

John Henry Newman's great prayer-hymn reflects that which is needed, not just in time of suicide or homicide, nor even just in the care of the convalescent mental patient, but in and beyond all of life as we know it on this planet.

> "Lead, kindly Light, amid th' encircling gloom,
>   Lead Thou me on;
>   The night is dark, and I am far from home;
>   Lead Thou me on:
>   Keep Thou my feet, I do not ask to see
>   The distant scene—one step enough for me."

16. Love Life and Let Live

There are times when convalescent mental patients need help in controlling their attitudes and actions. These have been detailed in earlier chapters of this book. For the most part, however, trying to control recovering patients is not helpful.

One of the causes of mental and emotional disorders has to do with the issue of who is going to control whom. Experts in the successful treatment of the mentally ill feel that many symptoms of mental illness are attempts by patients to gain control of their lives. In a sense, mental illness can be viewed in much the same way one views the behavior of children after the second year of life. They quickly seem to learn the word "NO," and use it often. Since they are so very young and need guidance and discipline, the "NO" must often be overlooked by parents. Parents should, of course, consider the child's protest. Often parents set high expectations and regulations which are not necessary.

For example, I know of one little boy whose parents refused to let him play in the mud, make mud pies, etc. So long as the mud is not contaminated by poison or the child has no open cuts into which germs may penetrate, playing in the mud does not harm children. This little boy's parents, however, just did not feel comfortable seeing him dirty, because *they* had been brought up to abhor dirt. They never realized how much fun a child can have playing in the mud.

One day the parents were horrified to discover that the little boy was saving his urine in an empty milk carton. When confronted with such crazy behavior, the little boy said, "Well, you told me I should not mix water with dirt to make mud, so I thought I'd try this."

The point of the story is that the needs and protests of small children need to be understood. In a similar way, people must realize that much of the "rebellion" of adolescents is actually a bid for independence. Rather than think only of punishment, we must comprehend the meaning of the rebellion when relating to adolescents.

The same is true in the care of convalescent mental patients. Except in extremely rare situations, usually of brief duration, mental patients are far more capable of handling their lives than we are apt to think. Protecting them from making (and learning from) mistakes, from "learning the hard way," does not help their convalescence.

Family and friends often wish to protect recovering patients from the full range of human experience. They seek to insulate patients from sorrow, excitement, fear, and even joy. They fear that "too much" weeping, thrill, fright, laughter, might cause the patient to regress.

Usually this is done out of love for the recovering patient. Patients experience this form of love differently. They experience it as being controlled. Overcontrol leads to a recurrence or an increase in the symptoms of mental illness. The best-intentioned controlling of the activity, diets, habits, friendships, work, etc., of recovering patients interfere with their complete recovery.

Mental patients gradually need to increase their ability to "make it" on their own. True love is neither clinging nor controlling. True love allows patients to make their own decisions. When they want help in controlling themselves, they will let you know directly or indirectly, as has been emphasized earlier in this book.

Lessons can be learned from the natural world of animals. Animals protect and care for, even control, as well as teach their young and their injured—up to a point. Then animals leave the young or the injured. They leave them, sometimes forcefully by kicking them out of the nest, sometimes by simply not following them when they go off on their own. In the savage "law of the jungle," most animals are thus freed to live. Sometimes they are freed to die if they cannot make it alone. As cruel as this may sound, freedom to fail, even to die "on one's own," is a more loving gift and affords greater dignity than overcontrol.

Before the recognition of the equal rights of women became popular in civilized countries, women were "given" in marriage. Despite the retention in many modern wedding services of the traditional phrase "Who giveth this woman to be married to this man?" most women in the United States are no longer "given in marriage" after arrangements have been made by parents. They are given the freedom to "fall in love" and to marry whom and as they choose. This naturally leads to mistakes, unhappy marriages, divorces, and "broken homes." But no more so than the older way led to happiness and fulfillment. Parents made and make mistakes also. Even in love. Perhaps the potential for fulfilled marriages and happy homes is also no greater than in the older way. But the new way, the way of giving freedom, has greater dignity and allows responsibility to rest where it belongs, on the free individual. Parents may sorrow when their children do not achieve fulfillment and joy, but they no longer need to feel the guilt of responsibility they never needed to assume.

With the care of the convalescent mental patient the same principles are appropriate. The patient, having attained reasonable ability to function, is shown love by being granted the right to decide for himself or herself who and what he or she shall be. They are "let go" to live, to survive, to attain security, and, it is hoped, to experience satisfaction. There is risk, of course. In this life there is always risk. There is also the promise of rewards that far outweigh the risk involved.

In Nazi Germany the mentally ill were scheduled for extinction. As the Gestapo approached, many mental institutions were unlocked by the medical and nursing personnel, and the patients were told to run for their lives. So many survived, despite the great risk!

In ancient Galilee there was a man, mentally ill by all our diagnostic standards, who was controlled by chains until he broke them and fled to a cemetery. There he lived in fear. People heard him crying out in the night. Then Jesus approached him. The man's fear turned to terror and he begged

Jesus not to torment him further. Jesus responded by treating the man, not as a maniac, but as a person. Jesus went through the formality of introductions, asking the man's name, treating the man as a human being. And the man was healed, by love, freed. Jesus let him live.

We do not live in Nazi Germany. We live in a nation established on the "inalienable rights" of all people, to "life, liberty, and the pursuit of happiness," based on Judeo-Christian beliefs.

Those who care for the convalescent mental patient may need help themselves as they learn anew the deeper meanings of love in order to relate to the patient that all may live—with freedom, taking risk, reaping reward, as God intends all to live. Or, as Jesus stated it, "that your joy may be full" (John 16:24).

Brief Bibliography of Writings by and Regarding Convalescent Mental Patients

Bennett, George. *When They Ask for Bread.* John Knox Press, 1978.

Boisen, Anton. *The Exploration of the Inner World.* Harper & Brothers, 1936.

Caplan, Gerald. *Principles of Preventive Psychiatry.* Basic Books, 1964.

Emotions Anonymous. International Services, P. O. Box 4245, St. Paul, Minnesota 55104.

Green, Hannah. *I Never Promised You a Rose Garden.* New American Library, 1964.

Mayer, Greta, and Hoover, Mary. *When Children Need Special Help with Emotional Problems.* A Child Study Association Publication, 1961.

Meyer, Adolf, "After-Care and Prophylaxis," in Alfred, Lief (ed.), *The Commonsense Psychiatry of Dr. Adolf Meyer.* McGraw-Hill Book Co., 1948. Pp. 300 ff.

Oates, Wayne E. *Religious Factors in Mental Illness:* Association Press, 1955.

Shneidman, Edwin S., and Mandelkorn, Philip. *How to Prevent Suicide.* Public Affairs Pamphlets, 1967.

Stern, Edith M. *Mental Illness, A Guide for the Family.* 2d rev. ed. National Association for Mental Health, 1957.

West, R. Frederick. *Light Beyond Shadows: A Minister and Mental Health.* Macmillan Co., 1959.